CEF Level **C1**

the
vocabulary
files

English Usage

Advanced

GlobalELT
ENGLISH LANGUAGE TEACHING BOOKS

CONTENTS

Unit 1	Page 3
Unit 2	Page 7
Unit 3	Page 11
Unit 4	Page 15
Unit 5	Page 19
Unit 6	Page 23
Unit 7	Page 27
Unit 8	Page 31
Unit 9	Page 35
Unit 10	Page 40
Unit 11	Page 46
Unit 12	Page 51
Unit 13	Page 55
Unit 14	Page 57
Unit 15	Page 61

Published by GLOBAL ELT LTD
www.globalelt.co.uk
email: orders@globalelt.co.uk
Copyright © **GLOBAL ELT LTD**

The right of Lawrence Mamas & Andrew Betsis to be identified as the authors of this work has been asserted in accordance with the Copyright, Designs and Patent Act 1988.

All rights reserved. No part of this publication may be reproduced, stored in a retrieval system, or transmitted in any form or by any means, electronic, mechanical, photocopying, recording or otherwise, without the prior permission in writing of the Publisher. Any person who does any unauthorised act in relation to this publication may be liable to criminal prosecution and civil claims for damages.

British Library Cataloguing-in-Publication Data

Components:
- Vocabulary Files - Level C1- Teacher's Book - ISBN: 978-1-904663-46-1
- Vocabulary Files - Level C1- Student's Book - ISBN: 978-1-904663-45-4

Unit 1

Words in Action

Adjectives showing courage

An **adventurous** person looks for adventure.
A **brave** one is self-confident in the presence of danger and ready to suffer pain.
A **chivalrous** man puts himself in danger for the protection of others.
A **bold** one stands out and faces danger bravely.
A **daring** one defies any dangers. A fearless person shows no fear.
An **intrepid** person possesses unshakable nerves.
A **courageous** person is more than brave, adding a moral element to his/her deeds.
An **audacious** person exhibits a fearless spirit, defiant even of law or decorum.
A **gallant** man is brave in a dashing and showy way.
A **valiant** person not only faces great dangers successfully but also achieves great results.

Exercise A >>> Complete the table with the noun derived from the corresponding adjective.

ADJECTIVES	NOUNS
adventurous	
brave	
chivalrous	
bold	
daring	

ADJECTIVES	NOUNS
fearless	
intrepid	
courageous	
audacious	
gallant	
valiant	

Exercise B >>> Read the text below and choose the correct word A, B C or D to fill the gaps.

CLOZE

Franklin Delano Roosevelt loved to travel, but not by air. A gregarious man who _____ (1) the company of other people, he preferred to go by rail or ship, savouring the _____ (2) and comfort that these familiar means of transport could provide a President of the United States with. His physical _____ (3), moreover, made flying difficult; the aircraft of the thirties and early forties were not _____ (4) to accommodate persons in wheelchairs. 'I'm in no hurry,' he once explained. 'The sooner I get where I'm going, the sooner people will be wanting something from me.' So, while Roosevelt _____ (5) in the White House longer than any President, he made only three trips by air during his entire time in office.

1. a avoided
   b relished
   c loathed
   d recognized

2. a leisure
   b hardships
   c rush
   d hassle

3. a obstacle
   b capacity
   c hindrance
   d handicap

4. a designed
   b done
   c promoted
   d thought

5. a evacuated
   b occupied
   c resided
   d prolonged

3

Vocabulary Development

Task One >>> Tick the word or phrase that appears closest to the meaning of the words in **bold**.

1 To **relish** means to ____ .   ☐ detest   ☐ like
2 **Hardships** cause ____ .   ☐ discomfort and suffering   ☐ advantages and opportunities
3 To **loathe** is to ____ .   ☐ dislike   ☐ enjoy
4 A **hostile** attitude is ____ .   ☐ friendly   ☐ unfriendly
5 A **bold** person is ____ .   ☐ shy   ☐ confident
6 An **illustrious** writer is ____ .   ☐ eminent   ☐ imminent
7 **In the event of rain** means ____ .   ☐ when the rain stops   ☐ in case it rains
8 A **skirmish** is ____ .   ☐ an open battle   ☐ a fight between small parts of armies

9 An **intriguing** story is ____ .   ☐ interesting   ☐ uninteresting
10 A person who **defies** the law ____ it.   ☐ obeys   ☐ disobeys
11 A beauty that **captivates** you ____ you.   ☐ fascinates   ☐ repulses
12 A **hindrance** is ____ .   ☐ whatever obstructs and delays you   ☐ whatever facilitates things for you

13 **Slack** discipline is ____ .   ☐ hard   ☐ relaxed
14 An **ingenious** young man is ____ .   ☐ clever   ☐ stupid
15 An **illiterate** person is ____ .   ☐ educated   ☐ unable to read

Task Two >>> What are the nouns derived from the adjectives listed below?

ADJECTIVES	NOUNS
significant	
cordial	
indecent	
obscure	
pious	
illiterate	

ADJECTIVES	NOUNS
hostile	
wise	
versatile	
flexible	
tolerant	
defiant	

Task Three >>> Complete the sentences using the words defined below.

A diseased - suffering from a disease ⇔ **deceased** - (person) who has recently died
Mr. Jones is no longer at this telephone number; I'm afraid he's _____ .

B locate - find the position of somebody or something ⇔ **localize** - confine to a particular part or area
I'm trying to _____ Shoreline Drive on the map, but I can't find it.

C luxurious - very rich and comfortable ⇔ **luxuriant** - abundant in vegetation
Their house was filled with _____ furnishings.

D eminent - distinguished ⇔ **imminent** - likely to happen soon
All the students were nervous about the _____ exams

E ingenious - clever & skillful (n. ingenuity) ⇔ **ingenuous** - not attempting to deceive or conceal; innocent (n. ingenuousness)
Mark has come up with an _____ plan to make a million dollars.

F capture - take a person or an animal prisoner   **captivate** - fascinate
The pirates managed to stop the ship and they _____ the captain and the crew.

G reign - rule ⇔ **rein** - a long narrow strap fastened to the bridle of a horse
She led the horse by the _____ .

H comment - give an opinion on something or someone ⇔ **commend** - praise
Don't you want to _____ on the political situation?

Task Four >>> Cross out the words in lists A and B which are not synonymous with the words in CAPITAL letters.

A ILLUSTRIOUS

- ☐ anonymous
- ☐ eminent
- ☐ obscure
- ☐ prominent
- ☐ outstanding
- ☐ imminent
- ☐ disreputable
- ☐ renowned
- ☐ renewed
- ☐ distinguished
- ☐ celebrated
- ☐ reputed

B MOROSE (for people)

- ☐ overcast
- ☐ sullen
- ☐ cordial
- ☐ sulky
- ☐ friendly
- ☐ amiable
- ☐ gloomy
- ☐ moody
- ☐ affable
- ☐ glum
- ☐ downcast
- ☐ courteous

Vocabulary Practice

A. Read the text below and choose the correct word A, B C or D to fit the gaps.

There can be no (11).................... that online shopping is of huge benefit to the consumer. Far from becoming (12)...................., online shoppers are very demanding. Overpriced merchants with poor services should beware. Gone are the days when stores could charge what they liked for goods and get away with it. The same, too, for shady manufacturers: smarter consumers know which products have a good (13).................... and which do not, because online they now read not only the sales (14).................... but also reviews from previous purchasers. And if customers are disappointed, a few (15).................... of the mouse will take them to places where they can let the world know. Nowadays there is nothing more damning than a flood of negative comments on the internet.

However, the big boys, as always, are ahead of the game. Some companies are already adjusting their business models to take account of these trends. The stores run by Sony and Apple, for instance, are more like brand showrooms than shops. They are there for people to try out (16).................... and to ask questions to knowledgeable staff. Whether the products are ultimately bought online or offline is of secondary importance.

Online traders must also adjust. Amazon, for one, is (17).................... turning from being primarily a bookseller to becoming a (18).................... retailer by letting other companies sell products on its site, rather like a marketplace. During America's Thanksgiving weekend last November, Amazon's sales of consumer electronics in the United States (19).................... its book sales for the first time in its history. Other transformations in the retail business are (20).................... to follow.

11. **A.** query **B.** examination **C.** question **D.** proposal
12. **A.** complacent **B.** dissatisfied **C.** competent **D.** compassionate
13. **A.** distinction **B.** resolution **C.** opinion **D.** reputation
14. **A.** bubble **B.** message **C.** blare **D.** blurb
15. **A.** taps **B.** clucks **C.** clicks **D.** prods
16. **A.** devices **B.** tools **C.** emblems **D.** schemes
17. **A.** mistakenly **B.** rapidly **C.** unreasonably **D.** secretly
18. **A.** mass **B.** block **C.** lump **D.** chunk
19. **A.** receded **B.** excluded **C.** repressed **D.** exceeded
20. **A.** tied **B.** secured **C.** bound **D.** fastened

B. Fill the gaps in the following sentences with the correct answer A, B C or D.

21 It was imperative for the authorities to .... the epidemic.
   a succeed   **b** localise   **c** spread   **d** define

22 His efforts, though futile, are still ....
   a refined   **b** intimidated   **c** pious   **d** commendable

23 To me friendship is a(n) .... thing.
   a precious   **b** insignificant   **c** costly   **d** obscure

24 He was reserved by nature, even ....
   a cordial   **b** morose   **c** amiable   **d** approachable

25 Misuse of the world's resources is one of the .... issues of our times.
   a burning   **b** heating   **c** firing   **d** boiling

26 That was an act of epic ....
   a validity   **b** price   **c** valour   **d** location

27 What he did to support our cause was a small but .... gesture.
   a significant   **b** stout   **c** obvious   **d** indecent

28 The vegetation on the island was ....
   a exuberant   **b** chivalrous   **c** overcast   **d** ingenious

29 He was regarded as the most .... of contemporary writers of fiction.
   a dense   **b** daring   **c** extensive   **d** imaginary

30 Ronald had the .... to blame his teachers for his failure.
   a concern   **b** chivalry   **c** regard   **d** audacity

Unit 2

Words in Action

Adjectives denoting physique

plump	fleshy or overweight	**lanky**	very thin, tall and ungraceful
corpulent	excessively fat	**spindly**	long, thin, suggesting weakness
obese	medically very overweight	**feeble**	weak, lacking in muscular power
muscular	strong with well-developed muscles	**delicate**	easily injured or easily made ill
stout	rather fat and heavy at the same time	**frail**	delicate, usually in poor health
hefty	big and strong	**gaunt**	thin, extremely weak, as though from lack of food
husky	strong and powerfully built	**sickly**	often ill
burly	large in body, bulky and stout	**bony**	very thin, as though the bones show through the skin
virile	exhibiting physical strength and sexual power	**skinny**	very thin
sturdy	possessing excellent health and strength	**decrepit**	weak and in bad condition from old age
robust	strong, healthy with stamina	**senile**	(connected with old age) showing the weakness of the body and especially of the mind

Exercise A >>> Complete the table with the noun derived from the corresponding adjective.

ADJECTIVES	NOUNS	ADJECTIVES	NOUNS
corpulent		stout	
obese		frail	
virile		senile	
decrepit		muscular	

Exercise B >>> Make three lists of adjectives that come under the headings of:

STRONG	FAT	WEAK

Vocabulary Development

Task One >>> Tick the one word or phrase that is closest in meaning to the word(s) in heavy type.

1. An **ex-convict** is a person
   - ☐ about to be punished
   - ☐ who has already undergone punishment

2. A **sane** individual is
   - ☐ healthy in mind
   - ☐ mad

3. A **naked** person
   - ☐ has his clothes on
   - ☐ hasn't got his clothes on

4. An enemy that **capitulates**
   - ☐ surrenders
   - ☐ fights to the bitter end

5. People who **abide by** the law
   - ☐ observe it
   - ☐ disregard it

6. An **unscrupulous** man
   - ☐ is guided by conscience
   - ☐ is not guided by conscience

7. A **graceful** woman
   - ☐ is attractive in movement
   - ☐ is unattractive in movement

8. A friend **sticking to** his promises
   - ☐ keeps them
   - ☐ breaks them

9. A **blunt** person
   - ☐ is invariably polite
   - ☐ doesn't take the trouble to be polite

10. A **convent** is another word for
    - ☐ monastery for women
    - ☐ school

Task Two >>> What are the nouns derived from the adjectives listed below?

ADJECTIVES	NOUNS
chivalrous	
treacherous	
poor	
prosperous	
royal	
sane	

ADJECTIVES	NOUNS
notorious	
loyal	
fit	
persistent	
noble	
cruel	

Task Three >>> Complete the sentences using the words defined below.

A **compulsive** - **very difficult to stop or control**
   compulsory - **something that must be done either by rules, laws, etc**
   A vision test is _____ when you are applying for a driver's license.

B **plump** - **slightly fat**
   plumber - **sb who fixes or installs water pipes, radiators, showers, etc.**
   Although Sharon is a bit _____ she still seems fit and healthy.

C **stout** - **rather fat and heavy**
   stately - **impressive and dignified**
   Who do you suppose lives in that _____ mansion?

D **in high spirits** - **cheerful and happy**
   in low spirits - **rather depressed**
   Jason was _____ for weeks after crashing his car.

E **capitulate** - **surrender on stated conditions; come to terms with the enemy and surrender**
   recapitulate - **go through the main points**
   Can you please _____ that for me; I'm not sure I understood.

F **vow** - **swear solemnly that one will do something**
   avow - **admit or declare openly**
   Will you _____ to stop smoking if I stop eating chocolate?

G **curtail** - **cut down/back on; reduce**
   entail - **make something necessary; involve**
   Don't agree to take on the job until you are sure what it _____ .

Task Four >>> Cross out the words in lists A and B which are **not** synonymous with the words in CAPITAL letters.

A CHIVALROUS

- ☐ corpulent
- ☐ gallant
- ☐ courteous
- ☐ courageous
- ☐ blunt
- ☐ robust
- ☐ honorable
- ☐ double-faced

B TREACHEROUS

- ☐ false
- ☐ disloyal
- ☐ faithful
- ☐ trustworthy
- ☐ dependable
- ☐ deceitful
- ☐ underhand
- ☐ reliable

9

Vocabulary Practice

A. Read the text below and choose the correct word **A, B C** or **D** to fit the gaps.

Greenhouse gases are being released into the atmosphere 30 times faster than the time when the Earth experienced a (11)............ episode of global warming. A study comparing the rate at which carbon dioxide and methane are being (12)............ now, compared to 55 million years ago when global warming also occurred, has found dramatic differences in the speed of release. James Zachos, professor of earth sciences at the University of California, Santa Cruz, said the speed of the present buildup of greenhouse gases is far greater than during the global warming after the (13)............ of the dinosaurs. "The emissions that caused this past episode of global warming probably lasted 10,000 years," Professor Zachos told the American Association for the Advancement of Science at a meeting in St. Louis. "By burning fossil fuels, we are likely to emit the same amount over the next three centuries." He warned that studies of global warming events in the geological past (14)............ the Earth's climate passes a (15)............ beyond which climate change accelerates with the help of positive feedbacks - vicious circles of warming. Professor Zachos is a leading (16)............ on the episode of global warming known as the palaeocene-eocene thermal maximum, when average global temperatures increased by up to 5ºC due to a massive release of carbon dioxide and methane.

His research into the deep ocean (17)............ suggests at this time that about 4.5 billion tons of carbon entered the atmosphere over 10,000 years. "This will be the same amount of carbon released into the atmosphere from cars and industrial emissions over the next 300 years if present (18)............ continue", he said. Although carbon can be released suddenly and naturally into the atmosphere from volcanic activity, it takes many thousands of years for it to be removed permanently by natural processes. The ocean is capable of removing carbon, and quickly, but this natural (19)............ can be easily (20)............, which is probably what happened 55 million years ago. "It will take tens of thousands of years before atmospheric carbon dioxide comes down to preindustrial levels," the professor said. "Even after humans stop burning fossil fuels, the effects will be long-lasting."

11. **A.** prearranged **B.** premier **C.** previous **D.** fundamental
12. **A.** emitted **B.** exhaled **C.** incorporated **D.** digested
13. **A.** dementia **B.** demolition **C.** detachment **D.** demise
14. **A.** comment **B.** mark **C.** compliment **D.** indicate
15. **A.** barricade **B.** verge **C.** threshold **D.** perimeter
16. **A.** autocrat **B.** authority **C.** administrator **D.** proprietor
17. **A.** dusts **B.** sediments **C.** dirt **D.** powder
18. **A.** trends **B.** gadgets **C.** fads **D.** crazes
19. **A.** capacity **B.** competence **C.** intelligence **D.** bulk
20. **A.** overcharged **B.** overstated **C.** overshadowed **D.** overwhelmed

B. Fill the gaps in the following sentences with the correct answer A, B C or D.

21 .... is a real health hazard.
   a Stupidity **b** Sturdiness **c** Animosity **d** Obesity
22 The old lady was becoming increasingly affected by ....
   a senility **b** masculinity **c** virility **d** chivalry
23 His .... excuses invariably exasperated the manager.
   a feeble **b** frail **c** robust **d** wealthy
24 I don't .... to be a genius but I am not stupid either.
   a permit **b** agree **c** compare **d** claim
25 Smoking can be .... to your health.
   a delightful **b** harmless **c** detrimental **d** indifferent
26 People .... their spending power when prices rise.
   a increase **b** curtail **c** prolong **d** think
27 He became an outlaw by .... the law.
   a defying **b** observing **c** sticking to **d** abiding by
28 .... is a punishable offense.
   a Hunting **b** Poaching **c** Jogging **d** Boxing
29 Marian was a beautiful, ... young lady.
   a corpulent **b** gaunt **c** slender **d** bony
30 Don't trust him; he's cruel, ... and unscrupulous.
   a loving **b** slack **c** treacherous **d** trustworthy

Unit 3

Words in Action

prevent	stop someone from doing something or something from being done
hinder	make more difficult for someone to do something or for something to happen e.g. *A snowstorm may prevent a train from running.* (the train does not run at all) or *A snowstorm may hinder the train from arriving on time.* 　(the train has actually run and arrived at its destination) You can equally *prevent the enemy from invading your country,* or *hinder the march of an enemy,* though you may not have enough force to oppose it.
obstruct	stop someone or something from moving forward by blocking their path e.g. *The road is obstructed by fallen trees.*
inhibit	make someone unable to express themselves freely e.g. *Her presence inhibited me from saying what I wanted to.*
stem	stop the flow or spread of something (usually liquid) e.g. *Pat pressure on the wound so as to stem the flow of blood.* 　*They believed they had a duty to stem the advance of the new sect.*
prohibit	forbid someone from doing something (usually by law or regulation) e.g. *Smoking is strictly prohibited.*
hamper	to make movement difficult e.g. *The long tight dress hampered her movements.*

Exercise A >>> Fill in the blanks in the following sentences with the appropriate word from the list above. You may use the same word more than once.

1. The advance of the rescue team was seriously _____ by the snowstorm.
2. This country has a law _____ young people from marrying before they come of age.
3. The terrible head-on collision of the trucks _____ traffic on the motorway for several hours.
4. His lisp _____ him from speaking freely.
5. Her tight skirt _____ her free movement.
6. The chief of police stressed the importance of _____ the inflow of illegal drugs into the city.
7. Business expansion is often _____ by bureaucracy.
8. To _____ the course of justice by withholding information is a serious penal offense.
9. The doctor tried to _____ the hemorrhage.
10. His presence _____ me from saying what I wanted to.
11. Her long illness _____ her progress at school.

Exercise B >>> Complete the table below with the correct form of the words that are missing.

VERB	ADJECTIVE	NOUN
prevent		
hinder		
	obstructive	
	inhibiting	
	prohibitive	

11

Vocabulary Development

Task One >>>
Tick the one word or phrase that is closest in meaning to the word(s) in heavy type.

1	A **fatally** injured driver	☐ succumbs to his injuries	☐ pulls through
2	To **convey** an idea is	☐ to prohibit it	☐ to make it known
3	A **boulder** is a	☐ large rock	☐ small rock
4	The **Infantry** is soldiers fighting	☐ on horseback	☐ on foot
5	A **penitentiary** is a	☐ mental institution	☐ prison
6	A **harsh** punishment is	☐ severe	☐ mild
7	When you **restrain** your anger,	☐ you keep it under control	☐ you increase it
8	What is **irksome** is	☐ annoying	☐ exciting
9	When somebody is taken **captive**, they are taken	☐ care of	☐ prisoner
10	When somebody **drifts** from one job to another, they	☐ stay put in the job	☐ often change jobs

Task Two >>>
In this exercise you have to combine each of the following pairs of sentences into one by omitting 'this'.
Each new sentence should include the noun derived from the word in heavy type.
Example: I see you are **unable** to do the job. This can't be overlooked.
Answer: Your inability to do the job can't be overlooked.

1 The lady was **obese**. This hampered her movements.
_____

2 They **scrutinised** the proposition. This led to their avoiding unnecessary expenditure.
_____

3 His lisp **impedes** his speech. This made it difficult for me to understand him.
_____

4 The judge is **impartial**. This is known to everybody.
_____

5 They **disclosed** their intentions. This made us shudder.
_____

6 His knowledge was **profound**. This astonished everyone present.
_____

7 He is **ingenious**. This can't be denied.
_____

8 He **departed** unexpectedly. This took me by surprise.
_____

9 He **committed** himself to helping us. This was a great relief.
_____

10 The people were utterly **destitute**. This aroused our sympathy.
_____

Task Three >>> Complete the sentences using the words defined below.

A **flavour (n)** - distinctive taste; special quality or characteristic
savour (v) - enjoy the taste or smell of sth
You couldn't possibly _____ your food when you eat so fast!

B **inhibit** - make somebody unable or unwilling to express his/her feelings
prohibit - forbid by law or regulation
His doctor _____ him from drinking alcohol.

C **implicit** - suggested rather than plainly stated
explicit - clearly and fully expressed
She didn't give _____ instructions, so she shouldn't be angry with you for doing it wrong.

D **superficial** - not thorough or profound
superfluous - more than needed or wanted
It is _____ to judge people by the clothes they wear.

E **pathetic** - causing one to feel sympathy
apathetic - showing a lack of interest in matters
Gregory has been _____ since he lost his job; he doesn't seem to want to do anything.

F **apprehend** - (legal) arrest, seize
comprehend - understand fully
I cannot _____ what caused her to act that way.

G **statute** - written law
stature - a person's body height
Although Jane is small in _____ she has a commanding personality.

H **induce** - persuade or influence
deduce - reach a conclusion by reasoning
Nothing could _____ him to move to the city.

Task Four >>> Each word in heavy type is **wrong** and requires **replacement**. Choose words from the box, and put them in the blanks.

| popular | humane | illicit | prone | stationery |
| inferred | ingenious | accessory | urban | descent |

1 I **implied** from what he said that he was in favor of my proposal. ....

2 It should be the duty of all of us to work for a more **human** and civilized society. ....

3 People with fair skin are **drone** to skin cancer. ....

4 The man in the courthouse was on trial for **elicit** smuggling of drugs. ....

5 The police held the firm belief that the suspect was an **access** to the crime. ....

6 He wrote a **populous** book and rose to fame. ....

7 The **dissent** of the mountain proved difficult. ....

8 We usually buy **stationary** in bulk for office use. ....

9 He's a versatile and **ingenuous** man. ....

10 Nowadays more and more people move to **urbane** areas. ....

Vocabulary Development

Task One >>> Tick the one word or phrase that is closest in meaning to the words in heavy type.

1 Another synonym for **beseech** is	☐ solicit	☐ elicit
2 A person going about in the **nude**	☐ has his clothes on	☐ has no clothes on
3 A **mere** detail is	☐ an unimportant one	☐ an important one
4 A **derogatory** remark	☐ shows respect	☐ shows no respect
5 When a marriage is **nullified** it is declared	☐ valid	☐ invalid
6 An **invalid** is a	☐ cripple	☐ healthy person
7 A **lawsuit** is a	☐ new suit of clothes	☐ court case
8 To **banish** somebody is to _____ him.	☐ praise	☐ exile
9 An accurate and **succinct** account is	☐ brief	☐ lengthy
10 A **divine** beauty is	☐ ordinary	☐ extraordinary
11 An **era** is a _____ period of time.	☐ long	☐ short

Task Two >>> Complete the sentences using the words defined below.

A **cute** - delightfully pretty and often small
  acute - sharp; penetrating
  Although their vision is poor, bats have a(n) _____ sense of hearing.

B **fierce** - violent; very great or strong
  pierce - make a hole through something with a pointed item
  The battle for the castle was _____ .

C **congenital** - (of a disease) existing from birth
  congenial - pleasant in agreement with one's taste
  Jack and Mary had a _____ conversation about their holiday plans.

D **contagious** - (of disease) spreading by contact
  contiguous - touching or neighboring
  Washing your hands frequently is the best way to avoid catching _____ illnesses.

E **snag** - any sort of difficulty or obstacle
  snug - cozy, warm and comfortable
  The elderly couple lived in a small, _____ cottage outside the village.

F **obscene** - morally disgusting; offensive
  obscure - not clearly seen or understood; unknown
  The museum houses famous paintings by Picasso and Monet as well as works by more _____ artists.

Task Three >>> Rewrite the following sentences to express the same meaning by changing the adjective in **bold** to an **adverb**. Make whatever changes are necessary.
Example: The doctor gave him a thorough examination. He was thoroughly examined by the doctor.

1 This is a **frequent** occurrence.
_____.

2 His intelligence was **remarkable**.
_____.

3 She has my **full** support.
_____.

4 Would you be so **kind** as to show me the way to the station?
_____?

5 It is not **possible** for me to sleep in a filthy place like this.
_____.

6 Despite his **serious** injury, he managed to get home.
_____.

7 The formality of his behavior was **absurd**.
_____.

8 She showed an **uncommon** interest in the new device.
_____.

9 There has been a **considerable** rise in prices lately.
_____.

10 He is **bad** at math.
_____.

Task Four >>> Fill each of the blanks with a suitable word or phrase from the box.

there's no him being	might as alone	meeting you would be on	action is taken really want	went to can (either)

1 'Why don't you trade in your old car for a new one?'
'I can't afford a new suit of clothes, let _____ a new car.'

2 'The first time we met was shortly after Christmas 2009.'
'I'm sorry, but I can't remember _____ before.'

3 Inflation will never be brought under control unless immediate _____ by the government.

4 I have to go to Boston tomorrow, but I don't _____ to.

5 'What's become of Joseph?' 'Well, I've had some bad news of _____ fired by the company.'

6 That's the restaurant we _____ during our holiday.

7 I can't help you and I don't think anyone else _____ .

8 I regret leaving my last job. I _____ a really good salary if I'd stayed.

9 'Would you like to go home now?' 'I _____ well, since my work's done.'

10 'Inflation gnaws at our income more and more every day.' 'Exactly, _____ denying the fact.'

17

Vocabulary Practice

A. Read the text below and choose the correct word A, B C or D to fit the gaps.

The Navajo are a peaceful and pastoral people, living by, with and off their flocks of sheep and goats. Though the arid character of their country - good for grazing only - forces them to **(11)**............... a nomadic life, most of the families have one main home, generally in a well-watered valley, where they raise corn, beans, melons, oats, alfalfa etc. The Navajo women weave the renown Navajo blankets, **(12)**............... for their durability, beauty and variety of design, and careful execution, whilst a number of men are clever silversmiths, making silver necklaces, belts, bracelets, wristlets, rings and buttons of rare beauty, out of Mexican silver dollars. They have always been self-sufficient. They have little of the sullen, reticent disposition **(13)**............... to Indians generally, and are cheerful, friendly, hospitable and industrious. Their government is democratic; there is no chief over the whole tribe, and their local chiefs are men of temporary and ill-defined authority, whose power **(14)**............... largely upon their personal influence, their eloquence and their reputation for wisdom and justice. The tribe is divided into about 58 clans or *gentes*, grouped under several original or nuclear clans. Marriages with Mexicans, Utes, Apaches, but especially with the neighbouring Pueblo Indians who were captured or enslaved and eventually adopted into the tribe, are responsible for a number of clans. As a **(15)**............... there is nothing like a pronounced or a prevailing Navajo type. Every variety of form and figure can be found among them. Marriage occurs early in life and polygamy and divorce are prevalent.

The elaborate system of pagan worship, expressed in chants, sacrifices, sand painting, dances, ceremonies, some of which last nine days, make the Navajo **(16)**............... very religious. Though they have no conception of one supreme being, their anthropomorphous deities are numerous and strikingly democratic. The ideas of heaven and hell being unknown to them, they believe in a hereafter **(17)**............... of a life of happiness with the people of the lower worlds. They are **(18)**............... believers in their faith system. Diseases are thought to be caused by evil beings, by malign influences of enemies, and by various occult agencies. Their remedies are largely magical and constitute an integral part of their religion. Their superstitions, ceremonies and customs are diligently kept alive by an extraordinarily large number of medicine men who **(19)**............... a powerful influence among them. Though missionaries have lived among the Navajo since the early 1600s, few Navajo have been **(20)**............... to Christianity.

11. **A.** hold   **B.** lead   **C.** serve   **D.** escort
12. **A.** notorious   **B.** famous   **C.** conspicuous   **D.** obscure
13. **A.** attributed   **B.** contributed   **C.** donated   **D.** blamed
14. **A.** reckons   **B.** determines   **C.** trusts   **D.** depends
15. **A.** connection   **B.** sequel   **C.** consequence   **D.** condition
16. **A.** assume   **B.** arise   **C.** appear   **D.** apply
17. **A.** containing   **B.** incorporating   **C.** blending   **D.** consisting
18. **A.** flimsy   **B.** firm   **C.** drastic   **D.** obstinate
19. **A.** wield   **B.** hang   **C.** fetch   **D.** process
20. **A.** converted   **B.** exchanged   **C.** confessed   **D.** modified

B. Fill the gaps in the following sentences with the correct answer A, B C or D.

21 Children under the age of 16 are not _____ to enter the competition.
    a eligible   **b** enabled   **c** legible   **d** promised

22 The driver's attention was _____ by a child running across the road.
    a deterred   **b** disturbed   **c** distracted   **d** destroyed

23 He's told us so many lies that we no longer place any _____ on what he says.
    a conviction   **b** reliance   **c** prediction   **d** reputation

24 His driving license has been _____ on the grounds of drink driving.
    a repealed   **b** revoked   **c** nullified   **d** recalled

25 The Conservatives declared their intention of _____ the whole Act once they came into power.
    a repulsing   **b** repelling   **c** impelling   **d** repealing

26 The problem of petty crime has largely been _____ .
    a annihilated   **b** exterminated   **c** eradicated   **d** decimated

27 Bacteria can't be seen by the _____ eye. You have to use a microscope.
    a nude   **b** naked   **c** bare   **d** mere

28 Mary is a(n) _____ liar. She was even arrested for lying to a police officer
    a physical   **b** congenital   **c** naive   **d** abnormal

29 Fortunately, everything went off without a _____ .
    a hope   **b** solution   **c** alternative   **d** hitch

30 The Prime Minister will decide whether to release the prisoner or not; that's his _____ .
    a prerogative   **b** derogatory   **c** abdication   **d** humanity

Unit 5

Words in Action

acid	unkind or critical	**tart**	sharp in manner
sour	having or showing a bad temper/ disagreeable in manner	**harsh**	severe, cruel, unsympathetic
bitter	hard to accept, usually used to express a feeling of disappointment/extremely cold	**cutting**	hurtful
		biting	sharply critical and is often caused by anger or dislike
caustic	sarcastic		

Exercise A >>> Choose either a, b or c to complete each sentence.

1 There was little protection against the _____ wind.
   a bitter   **b** powerless   **c** sour

2 It is sometimes very difficult to appreciate his _____ wit.
   a caustic   **b** nieve   **c** frail

3 Josh's _____ irony is just a means of making him feel superior.
   a decrepit   **b** intrepid   **c** cutting

4 The professor, weary and increasingly _____ in mood, walked into the auditorium.
   a valiant   **b** biting   **c** sour

5 I'm sure that his _____ remarks and sarcasm were a result of your own hostile behavior towards him.
   a biting   **b** gentle   **c** robust

6 I have often felt hurt by her _____ humor.
   a annihilating   **b** acid   **c** courageous

7 Her _____ reply left us shocked at her insolent behaviour.
   a hefty   **b** delicate   **c** tart

8 It has often been found that _____ punishment in many cases proves to be detrimental rather than beneficial.
   a caustic   **b** cutting   **c** harsh

9 Failing their senior class was a _____ disappointment for many students.
   a gallant   **b** feeble   **c** bitter

10 She was often reduced to tears by her tutor's _____ remarks.
   a harsh   **b** gaunt   **c** luxuriant

Exercise B >>> Put the correct word in the sentences below using the corresponding words on the right.

1 She's the _____ head of the company.
2 She's a _____ young woman.   **VIRTUAL - VIRTUOUS**

3 She was rather large and _____.
4 Her _____ courage inspired us all.   **UNFAILING - UNGAINLY**

5 Don't touch these tools! They're not your _____.
6 Mary behaves with perfect _____.   **PROPERTY - PROPRIETY**

7 He lives in _____ fear of being discovered.
8 Daffodils are _____ plants.   **PERENNIAL - PERPETUAL**

9 He _____ his rare collection of old coins.
10 The truth is that he _____ the challenge of competition.   **RELISHES - CHERISHES**

11 He was neither happy nor _____ about what happened.
12 His behaviour at the party was most _____.   **REGRETFUL - REGRETTABLE**

19

Vocabulary Development

Task One >>> Tick the word or phrase that best completes each sentence.

1 A **profitable** business ____ .
☐ makes a profit   ☐ makes no profit

2 **Labor** is very ____ work.
☐ hard   ☐ easy

3 Another synonym for **slaughter** is ____ .
☐ slay   ☐ prey

4 The opposite of **debtor** is ____ .
☐ credible   ☐ creditor

5 To **enslave** is to ____ somebody.
☐ subjugate   ☐ irritate

6 When you **initiate** direct talks with somebody, you ____ them.
☐ start   ☐ terminate

7 A **benevolent** society ____ the needy.
☐ helps   ☐ ignores

8 When old fashioned cars are **superseded** by catalytic cars ____ .
☐ the former take the place of the latter   ☐ the latter take place of the former

9 When there's a long standing **feud** between two people it means that they ____ .
☐ are on good terms   ☐ hate each other

Task Two >>> Complete the sentences using the words defined below.

A **wary** - be careful about something ⇔ **weary** - extremely tired

He's been _____ of dogs since he was bitten.

B **stinging** - bitter, unkind ⇔ **stringent** (of rules) severe

The job advertisement listed many _____ requirements.

C **renovate** - repair and return to good condition ⇔ **innovate** - introduce something new; make changes

It is a great deal of work to _____ a house.

D **implicit** - not directly expressed ⇔ **explicit** - clearly and fully expressed

It is _____ that you will dress up if you go to a wedding.

E **status** - a person's social, legal or professional position ⇔ **statute** - a written law

Some people feel that a new car can increase their _____ .

F **utility** - usefulness ⇔ **utilisation** - making use of something or finding a use for something

The efficient _____ of time is an important skill to learn.

Task Three >>>
Rewrite the following sentences or join them by using the **NOUN** derived from the words in **bold**.
*Example: They **predicted** the results amazingly accurately.*
Answer: Their PREDICTION of the results was amazingly accurate.

1 We can't easily **dispose** of nuclear waste.
_____.

2 Without a doubt he was **devoted** to his wife.
_____.

3 The supplies were **inadequate**. This resulted in the failure of the expedition.
_____.

4 That it was an **insane** notion needed no questioning.
_____.

5 His **inept** remark exasperated everybody present.
_____.

6 We should duly emphasize how **immediate** the problem is.
_____.

7 They **deferred** payment due to lack of funds.
_____.

8 You can't take her **frivolous** remark seriously.
_____.

9 He acted astonishingly **fast**.
_____.

10 The lack of books impoverishes us **intellectually**.
_____.

Task Four >>> Fill in the blanks with appropriate **prepositions**.

1 'Your father looks busy, doesn't he?'   'He's working _____ a new book; his autobiography, actually.'
2 'How badly was the car damaged?'   'The damage _____ it was terrible.'
3 'Do you know him?'   'We do know him _____ sight, you might say, but not very well.'
4 'How soon will the new model be available?'   'It will be _____ sale from next month on.'
5 'What are you looking for?'   'The scissors! What have you done _____ them?'
6 'Shall I drive you to the airport?'   'No, thanks, I'd rather go _____ my car.'
7 'They dress well, don't they?'   'They can afford to; they're well _____, you know.'
8 'Why are they demolishing the front of the building?'
   'They're making _____ the ground floor flat into a shop, I think.'
9 'Could I speak to Dr. Jenkins, please?'   'Hold on a moment. I'll put you _____ to him.'
10 'Do I stand a chance of passing the exam, sir?'
   'You do! Put your best foot forward and don't let me _____.'

Vocabulary Practice

A. Read the text below and choose the correct word A, B C or D to fit the gaps.

As petrol prices continue to **(11)**............. , many people are looking for ways to reduce the **(12)**............. of higher prices while still doing the driving necessary to their work and other activities. **(13)**............. are some suggestions which will save you a **(14)**............. amount of money on petrol.

1. Ask yourself every time you **(15)**............. to use your car, truck, SUV, or van, "Is this trip really necessary?" Every mile you drive your vehicle will cost you at least an **(16)**............. of 36 cents. If the trip is not necessary, think twice before using your vehicle.

2. Drive at a **(17)**............. speed on the motorway. According to the Department of Energy, most automobiles get about 20 percent more miles per gallon on the motorway at 55 miles per hour than they do at 70 miles per hour.

3. Consider **(18)**............. an automobile which gets the best petrol mileage. For example, generally, the following get better petrol mileage: lighter weight vehicles, vehicles with smaller engines, vehicles with manual transmissions, those with four cylinders, and those with fewer accessories. Check the "fuel economy" labels **(19)**............. to the windows of new automobiles to find the average estimated miles per gallon for given makes and models.

4. Decrease the number of short trips you make. Short trips **(20)**............. reduce petrol mileage. If an automobile gets 20 miles per gallon in general, it may get only 4 miles per gallon on a short trip of 5 miles or less.

11. **A.** crash	**B.** accelerate	**C.** escalate	**D.** fly
12. **A.** danger	**B.** occurrence	**C.** burden	**D.** chance
13. **A.** Below	**B.** After	**C.** Coming	**D.** Later
14. **A.** measurable	**B.** negotiable	**C.** negligible	**D.** considerable
15. **A.** think	**B.** plan	**C.** need	**D.** arrange
16. **A.** equivalent	**B.** average	**C.** amount	**D.** increase
17. **A.** mild	**B.** conservative	**C.** considerate	**D.** substantial
18. **A.** inquiring	**B.** trading	**C.** preferring	**D.** purchasing
19. **A.** attached	**B.** selected	**C.** stretched	**D.** held
20. **A.** extensively	**B.** exclusively	**C.** intensively	**D.** drastically

B. Fill the gaps in the following sentences with the correct answer A, B C or D.

21 This road is ____ to floods in winter.
   a fragile **b** sensitive **c** leading **d** unprotected

22 The new town development has begun to ____ on the surrounding green belt.
   a reach **b** encroach **c** enter **d** intrude

23 I was informed by the police officer that he would be forced to take me into ____.
   a guardianship **b** bail **c** custody **d** protection

24 My inquiries did not ____ any information of value.
   a elicit **b** arouse **c** illicit **d** swell

25 Charles was not sure which profession to enter, but finally ____ for law.
   a chose **b** opted **c** accepted **d** selected

26 His ____ sarcasm exasperated me.
   a biting **b** decorous **c** benevolent **d** fearful

27 His ____ as a brave soldier spread throughout the country.
   a renovation **b** renown **c** pilgrimage **d** expedition

28 He found it all but impossible to bear the ____ of a nomadic life.
   a amenities **b** sourness **c** decorum **d** harshness

29 He ____ the illusion that he will live to be a hundred.
   a grows **b** relishes **c** develops **d** cherishes

30 Samantha was dressed in a very ____ trouser suit.
   a contemptible **b** decorous **c** stinging **d** becoming

Unit 6

Words in Action

A **blow** is a violent stroke given by the hand or weapon (to somebody or something). It also means a sudden shock or disaster for somebody or something.
   e.g. He dealt him a blow on the head.
   His death came as a blow to the family.

A **misfortune** carries the idea of bad luck, often of a serious nature. It is usually of a lingering character or consequence, and such that the sufferer is not considered directly responsible. **e.g.** He had the misfortune to be born blind.

An **adversity** is an unfortunate event or unfavorable situation, usually caused by outward circumstances such as the loss of fortune, position, etc.

A **calamity** is a serious misfortune or disaster causing a great deal of damage, destruction or suffering.

A **hardship** is a specific difficult condition of life such as lack of food, comfort, money, etc.

A **mishap** conveys the idea of a minor and unfortunate accident.

A **reverse** is any change or alteration for the worse.

Distress is a state or condition of great suffering, danger, anxiety, pain or discomfort.

Affliction denotes the state of physical or mental suffering.

A **trial** (to somebody) is a troublesome or irritating person that must be endured.

A **stroke** can be any blow or ill effect caused as if by a blow, such as a stroke of misfortune or sunstroke. It can also be an attack of paralysis or apoplexy.

NOTE
For the loss of friends by death we commonly use **blow**, **affliction** or **bereavement**.
We speak of the **misery** of the poor,
the **hardships** of the soldier,
the **misfortunes** of a businessman,
the **adversities** met with because of bad weather,
the **calamities** of war,
a **mishap** preventing you from doing something,
people in **distress**, and
a boy being a **trial** to his mother.

Exercise >>> Choose the correct word in the parenthesis to complete each sentence below.

1. My uncle's sudden inability to move was diagnosed as a paralytic _____. (stroke/blow)
2. Sorry we're late, but we had a little _____ (mishap/misfortune) on the way here. We got a flat tyre on the highway.
3. Paralysis is a terrible _____. (affliction/adversity)
4. The two drunken sailors kicked up a brawl and exchanged _____ (strokes/blows) outside the tavern.
5. Towards the end of the experiment, the subjects showed signs of great _____. (hardship/distress)
6. The recent floods were the worst _____ (calamity/mishap) in the country's history.
7. The mischievous boy was a _____ (trial/misfortune) to his parents and teachers alike.
8. The _____ (afflictions/hardships) borne by explorers during the expedition resulted in their relinquishing any hope of conquering the unknown territory.
9. The captain had the _____ (mishap/misfortune) to hit an iceberg on his maiden voyage.
10. The airline had lost her suitcase; the customs officer had misplaced her passport. Yet, despite all this, she remained cheerful in the face of her _____. (adversities/misfortunes)
11. He suffered many _____ (reverses/strokes) in his political career.

Vocabulary Development

Task One >>> Tick the one word or phrase that is closest in meaning to the words in heavy type.

1 People living in **squalid** living conditions live in ____.
  - ☐ wretched conditions
  - ☐ clean conditions

2 A **derelict** house is ____.
  - ☐ ramshackle and run-down
  - ☐ posh and well-constructed

3 If you are **hard up** you ____.
  - ☐ have enough money
  - ☐ don't have enough money

4 A **jerry-built** house is ____.
  - ☐ well constructed
  - ☐ badly constructed

5 A **poor** person is ____.
  - ☐ indigent and destitute
  - ☐ wealthy and affluent

6 A **mishap**, such as losing one's scarf, is a ____.
  - ☐ serious misfortune
  - ☐ minor misfortune

7 A **mischievous** boy behaves in a way people ____.
  - ☐ approve of
  - ☐ disapprove of

8 **Downtrodden** people are invariably ____.
  - ☐ oppressed
  - ☐ pampered

9 A **brawl** is a ____, usually in a public place.
  - ☐ discussion
  - ☐ fight

10 When you prove your **mettle**, you show you are ____ to do things.
  - ☐ able
  - ☐ unable

11 When you **relinquish** a privilege or a claim, you ____.
  - ☐ put it forward
  - ☐ give it up

12 A point **vital** to an argument is ____ to it.
  - ☐ important
  - ☐ unimportant

Task Two >>> What are the nouns derived from the words listed below?

	NOUN
convert	
destitute	
indignant	

	NOUN
mischievous	
indict	
vital	

	NOUN
subvert	
indigent	
condemn	

Task Three >>> Complete the sentences using the words defined below.

A **indigent** - poor ⇔ **indigenous** - native; belonging naturally to a place
The pigeon is not _____, it was brought here by people.

B **diligent** - hard working; studious; industrious ⇔ **indolent** - lazy; idle
He is a _____ student and always start preparing well before an exam.

C **adversity** - a considerable disappointment, failure or misfortune ⇔
adversary - an enemy or opponent
I hear they had a great time cycling across Africa, even though they had to overcome many _____ .

D **afflict** - cause trouble, pain or distress ⇔
inflict - cause somebody to suffer by imposing something on him/her
Anna won't be at work this week because she is _____ with the measles.

E **rush** - move quickly ⇔ **rash** - acting or done without careful thought, especially of the consequences
Don't you think it's _____ of Jodie to accept the job in China without even visiting first?

F **avert** - turn away; avoid ⇔ **divert** - when sb diverts your attention from sth important you disapprove of them behaving in a way that stops you thinking about it.
He can't stand the sight of blood and always _____ his eyes in violent movies.

G **convert** - change into another form or use; cause somebody to change his/her religious beliefs ⇔
subvert - try to destroy the power and influence of a government or established ideas, beliefs, etc
See that man in the suit? He is trying to _____ passers-by to the Mormon religion.

Task Four >>> Choose from the correct words in parenthesis to complete the sentences below.

Academic freedom is based on the principle that the **1)**_____ (**function** / **fraction**) of an institution of higher learning is to increase and preserve knowledge, evaluate it, and **2)**_____ (**impair** / **impart**) it to others.

For the institution to **3)** _____ (**perform** / **carry**) this function, its scholars must be free to **4)**_____ (**do** / **hold**) and express views which at times can be unpopular or **5)**_____ (**even** / **much**) mistaken, **6)**_____ (**which** / **for**) it is only through an open exchange of varying points of view that ideas can be tested and knowledge **7)**_____ (**advanced** / **commenced**).

However, **8)**_____ (**conflicting** / **inflicting**) interpretations of the limits and **9)**_____ (**prohibitions** / **negotiations**) of academic freedom have often led to **10)**_____ (**displays** / **disputes**) between teachers and the governing boards of educational institutions.

25

Vocabulary Practice

A. Read the text below and choose the correct word A, B C or D to fit the gaps.

The New England Forestry foundation, (NEFF) now has a place it can use to showcase sustainable forestry. It wasn't easy and NEFF still needs to **(11)**............... £2.2 million to complete the capital campaign. The Prouty property has been a fixture in the landscape of Littleton for almost a century. In 2002, Donald Prouty, former Littleton town Moderator and town counsel **(12)**............... . Landvest was engaged to sell the property. Recognizing the opportunity to protect a significant tract of forestland within the rapidly **(13)**............... U.S. Route 495 corridor, Landvest introduced NEFF to the property. After walking the property and meeting with representatives of the town, NEFF boldly signed a purchase and sale agreement with the Prouty family. The family generously agreed to a bargain sale price in order to preserve the property and avoid a likely **(14)**............... war among developers. Valued in **(15)**............... of £3 million, the family's generous offer demonstrated their commitment to conserving the property. In October 2003, NEFF **(16)**............... financing at a highly competitive rate and purchased the property. This wonderful community resource was dedicated "Prouty Woods community forest" at a dedication ceremony in October 2004.

NEFF now provides public **(17)**............... throughout the property and educational opportunities at the William A. King Education Center, located at the top of Wilderness Hill. NEFF continues to manage the land as an active working forest - as Don and Carey Prouty had done for years. **(18)**............... from Fay Park to Long Lake, the 107-acre Prouty property is a truly unique and significant tract of woodland within minutes of Route 495. The property includes 1600 feet of frontage on Long Lake and the top of Wilderness Hill offers expansive views to the west and north including Mount Monadnock in New Hampshire. The combination of forest, hayfield and riparian zones provide much-needed habitat for a variety of species. The forest has been under professional forest management for many years. Walking trails maintained by the Littleton Conservation Trust connect to a town-wide system of walking trails. The town has protected significant acreage at Long Lake Park and along the **(19)**............... of Long Lake across from the Prouty property. The town-owned Morgan property adjoins to the north. In addition, the town has purchased a conservation restriction on 85 acres of Prouty Woods Community Forest, further increasing the conservation **(20)**............... of this property.

11. **A.** lift   **B.** elevate   **C.** promote   **D.** raise
12. **A.** gave away   **B.** passed away   **C.** passed off   **D.** gave over
13. **A.** developing   **B.** devising   **C.** deriving   **D.** deviating
14. **A.** bidding   **B.** proposing   **C.** letting   **D.** summoning
15. **A.** extra   **B.** over   **C.** excess   **D.** profit
16. **A.** attached   **B.** tightened   **C.** secured   **D.** possessed
17. **A.** passage   **B.** acclaim   **C.** entrant   **D.** access
18. **A.** Stretching   **B.** Swelling   **C.** Pushing   **D.** Multiplying
19. **A.** coast   **B.** shore   **C.** verge   **D.** hem
20. **A.** fee   **B.** value   **C.** prize   **D.** treasure

B. Fill the gaps in the following sentences with the correct answer A, B C or D.

21 Mr. Connors was _____ at the police station for further questioning.
   a restrained   **b** detained   **c** contained   **d** taken

22 I don't know how on earth he can get by on such _____ wages.
   a meager   **b** adequate   **c** satisfactory   **d** high

23 Don't read in such dim light; it will _____ your eyesight.
   a impair   **b** dwindle   **c** decrease   **d** contract

24 The gift was a _____ of his gratitude.
   a segment   **b** specimen   **c** receipt   **d** token

25 They were able to set sail when the storm _____.
   a enraged   **b** abated   **c** shrank   **d** permitted

26 I'd love to live in these _____ surroundings.
   a desolate   **b** bashful   **c** gloomy   **d** serene

27 This kind of occupation does not offer any _____ for creative thinking.
   a orbit   **b** rope   **c** scope   **d** infection

28 Mr. Smithers _____ to comment on the news.
   a upheld   **b** retained   **c** declined   **d** decreased

29 Law-abiding people are the people who _____ the law.
   a observe   **b** offend   **c** protect   **d** defy

30 The number of people going to soccer matches seems to be _____ steadily.
   a narrowing   **b** withering   **c** dwindling   **d** contracting

Unit 8

Words in Action

Exercise A >>> Match the words on the left with their definitions on the right.

PART A:
1. abate
2. adroit
3. accost
4. aggravate
5. arrogance

- ☐ make worse and more serious
- ☐ subside; become less in intensity
- ☐ haughtiness
- ☐ skillful; clever
- ☐ meet and speak to sb in a way that seems rude

PART B:
1. brim
2. chaste
3. defect
4. demolish
5. commence

- ☐ become an apostate
- ☐ the upper edge, as of a glass
- ☐ begin; start
- ☐ morally pure
- ☐ tear down

Exercise B >>> Fill in the blanks with the correct word, a, b, c or d.

1. I bumped into John in Athens and he _____ me before I had time to speak first.
   a accosted   b ajar   c brawled   d jolted

2. He's very whimsical; he does things on the _____ of the moment.
   a brim   b spur   c clap   d push

3. He slipped and fell and _____ his wrist.
   a aroused   b flushed   c sprained   d chaste

4. The doctor warned him that if he continued to pick the sore he would _____ it.
   a demolish   b designate   c exasperate   d aggravate

5. The board president designated a _____ team to tear down the dilapidated building which jeopardised the passers-by.
   a demolition   b castigating   c contaminating   d drenching

6. The corrupt politician was bribed to _____ to the opposing party.
   a perfect   b defect   c infect   d reflect

7. I detest that _____ know-it-all expression on his face.
   a bewildered   b arduous   c arrogant   d complexity

8. The Secretary of State handled the matter _____ and prevented a war.
   a adroitly   b intensely   c abjectly   d slightly

9. As soon as the storm _____, the ships will be allowed to set sail.
   a abets   b abates   c forbids   d incites

10. Let's hurry to the theater. The play is to _____ at eight o'clock sharp.
    a commend   b recommend   c commence   d comment

31

Vocabulary Development

Task One >>> Complete the sentences using the words defined below.

A **thrive** - prosper ⇔ **strive** - try hard
The stray cat she adopted will _____ now that it has enough food.

B **sustain** - keep up; maintain; support ⇔ **retain** - keep or continue to have something
The city _____ minor damage during the earthquake.

C **yoke** - servitude or slavery ⇔ **yolk** - the yellow part of an egg
The egg _____ is very nutritious.

D **document** - any written or printed matter that provides evidence ⇔
documentary - cinema or T.V. film showing aspects of human or animal life and social activities
They watched a _____ on the Amazon rain forest.

E **constrain** - make sb do sth by using force or persuasion ⇔ **restrain** - keep under control
That dog is a hazard and should be _____ .

F **soothe** - calm ⇔ **seethe** - be agitated; extremely angry
Try this cream; it will _____ your sunburn.

G **subside** - sink to a lower level ⇔ **subsidize** - help financially
It took a long time for his grief to _____ after his grandmother died..

Task Two >>> Rewrite each of the sentences below by replacing the words in **bold** with an appropriate phrase using the verb in **CAPITALS**. Make whatever other changes are necessary.

Example: *We must **end** all this vandalism and destruction caused by hooligans.* **(PUT)**
Answer: *We must put an end to all this vandalism and destruction caused by hooligans.*

1 Most of my friends **prefer** baseball. (HAVE)

2 It is high time we **acted** positively. (TAKE)

3 Huge crowds **gathered** for the procession. (TURN)

4 He didn't **appear** until much later. (PUT)

5 The war **ended** in 1945. (COME)

6 They **considered** his previous sales experience before taking him on the staff. (TAKE)

7 An architect **surveyed** the house before it was bought. (MAKE)

8 The firm has **fitted** safety belts in all its vehicles. (EQUIP)

9 How can he **manage** on his poor salary? (GET)

10 He decided to stop **attending** the college and get a job. (DROP)

Task Three >>> Underline the one word in the parenthesis that best completes each sentence.

1 I knew from the (onslaught - onset) that the plan would turn out to be a flop.
2 Now, what's the (snag - snug)?
3 A clumsy driver may even collide with a (stationary - stationery) vehicle.
4 No reverse could (deter - defer) him from proceeding.
5 This is the fifth (successive - successful) game they've won this month.
6 What an (inventive - eventful) day it has been.
7 Austere measures mean practising (frigid - rigid) economics.
8 He was in a (trivial - jovial) mood that day.
9 Malaria is a (contiguous - contagious) disease.
10 Do you know how to (steer - stir) the boat?
11 He suffered many (reserves - reverses) throughout his life.
12 They live in a (choosy - cosy) little house.

Task Four >>> Replace the words in heavy type with a single word from the box with the same meaning.

| stabilisers | drought | imminent | identification | scope | unpredictable |
| prospering | nepotism | espionage | entail | precarious | |

1 I judged from the state of the sky that a thunderstorm was **coming on**. _____
2 Most modern ships are fitted with **devices intended to keep them on an even keel**. _____
3 People who are found guilty of **the practice of spying** _____ are put in jail.
4 Tom's character was **such that no one could tell what he would do next**. _____
5 Throughout history, many politicians have been guilty of **handing out high offices to their relations**. _____
6 Hilary's business is **doing exceptionally well**. _____
7 Astrophysics is a subject beyond the **range of action and ability** of my mind _____.
8 Last year's crop failed due to **dry weather and lack of rainfall**. _____
9 Cheating in the exam may **have as a result** _____ your disqualification.
10 The company's position is **far from safe**. _____
11 The police officer stopped the suspicious looking man in the State Department, and asked for **papers that could prove who he was**. _____

Vocabulary Practice

A. Read the text below and choose the correct word A, B C or D to fit the gaps.

Despite the continued (11)........................ of those early town perks, it wasn't until the Depression that modern Hershey started to take shape. Perhaps the only town in the country actually to (12)........................ during the 1930s, it thrived because Hershey vowed his Utopia would never see a breadline. Instead he (13)........................ a massive building boom that gave rise to the most visited buildings in today's Hershey and delivered wages to more than 600 workers. He admitted that his (14)........................ were partly selfish: "If I don't provide work for them, I'll have to feed them. And since building materials are now at their lowest cost levels, I'm going to build and give them jobs."
He seems to have (15)........................ no expense; most of the new buildings were strikingly (16)........................ . The first to be finished was the three-million-dollar limestone Community Center, home to the 1,904-seat Venetian-style Hershey Community Theater, which has played (17)........................ since 1933 to touring Broadway shows and to music, dance, and opera performances. It offers just as much to look at when the lights are on and the curtains closed. The floors in the (18)........................ named Grand Lobby are polished Italian lava rock, surrounded by marble walls and capped with a bas-relief ceiling showing sheaves of wheat, beehives, swans, and scenes from Roman mythology. With the (19)........................ inner foyer, Hershey thumbed his nose even harder at the ravages of the Depression: The arched ceiling is tiled in gold, the fire curtain bears a painting of Venice, and the ceiling is (20)........................ with 88 tiny lightbulbs to re-create a star-lit night.

11. **A.** flexibility	**B.** rigidity	**C.** elasticity	**D.** resilience
12. **A.** prosper	**B.** decline	**C.** get on	**D.** flower
13. **A.** trusted	**B.** funded	**C.** accounted	**D.** stocked
14. **A.** pretensions	**B.** objections	**C.** preoccupation	**D.** intentions
15. **A.** spared	**B.** spent	**C.** allowed	**D.** justified
16. **A.** impoverished	**B.** unattractive	**C.** poor	**D.** opulent
17. **A.** hosting	**B.** housing	**C.** host	**D.** homogeneously
18. **A.** aptly	**B.** inappropriately	**C.** seemingly	**D.** frightfully
19. **A.** dizzying	**B.** gaudy	**C.** dazzling	**D.** bland
20. **A.** holed	**B.** studded	**C.** supported	**D.** magnified

B. Fill the gaps in the following sentences with the correct answer A, B C or D.

21 Employees who have a _____ are encouraged to discuss it with the management.
   a hindrance   **b** grievance   **c** disturbance   **d** precaution

22 Decrepitude seriously _____ vision and hearing.
   a impairs   **b** enhances   **c** withers   **d** shrinks

23 They _____ his proposal before accepting it.
   a rejected   **b** ignored   **c** overlooked   **d** scrutinised

24 A few political extremists _____ the crowd to attack the police.
   a incited   **b** animated   **c** stirred   **d** agitated

25 He spent his entire life _____ round the world, never settling down.
   a scattering   **b** roaming   **c** exploring   **d** transporting

26 The examiner's cold stare _____ Mary.
   a amazed   **b** dumbfounded   **c** imperiled   **d** disconcerted

27 It's high time we _____ the procedure.
   a tortured   **b** occurred   **c** commenced   **d** soothed

28 The judge decided to _____ the trial till the following week.
   a admire   **b** admit   **c** adjust   **d** adjourn

29 I wouldn't like to _____ my good name and reputation.
   a enrich   **b** jeopardise   **c** constrain   **d** prolong

30 If I was to do that, it would _____ my employer's displeasure.
   a occur   **b** incur   **c** recur   **d** concur

Unit 9

Words in Action

Exercise A >>> Match Column I with Column II (Synonyms) and Column III (Opposites).

Column 1	Column 2	Column 3
1 alluring	___ harmful; noxious	___ cool; collected
2 deteriorate	___ digressive; deviating	___ tidy; neat
3 cheeky	___ despicable; loathsome	___ repellent; repugnant
4 fetid	___ attractive; tempting	___ aromatic; fragrant
5 detrimental	___ slipshod; slatternly	___ steadfast; stable
6 rattled	___ fickle; capricious	___ beneficial; salutary
7 abhorrent	___ stinking; offensive	___ affable; civil
8 slovenly	___ insolent; rude; blunt	___ lovable; amiable
9 discursive	___ impair; degenerate	___ coherent; connected
10 whimsical	___ confused; embarrassed	___ improve; ameliorate

Exercise B >>> Fill in the blanks with the correct word, a, b, c or d.

1 His behavior is horrible; even his family _____ him.
   a adore   b abhor   c admire   d allure

2 I can't bear _____ in a child. Her cheek will not go unpunished.
   a decency   b obedience   c respect   d audacity

3 Firemen must be _____ in the face of danger.
   a alluring   b bald   c darling   d daring

4 A _____ breath is often an indication of dental cavities.
   a fragrant   b aromatic   c defensive   d fetid

5 He studied _____; hence he passed his test hands down.
   a relatively   b slovenly   c diligently   d lazily

6 It's not enough to swelter in this _____ weather; we've got smog to boot.
   a chilly   b sultry   c discursive   d pensive

7 Never be _____ and ask a woman how old she is.
   a affable   b false   c acute   d indiscreet

8 Her condition seems to be _____. We'll have to take her to intensive care.
   a ameliorating   b deteriorating   c amputating   d imitating

9 The girl playfully ran away, but before she disappeared round the corner, she turned and gave us a ___ smile.
   a valuable   b musical   c despicable   d whimsical

10 The lawyer's aggressive questioning seemed to _____ the witness on the stand.
   a rattle   b battle   c stable   d ladle

Vocabulary Development

Task One >>> Rewrite the following sentences to express the same meaning by replacing the word in **bold** with an **ADJECTIVE** derived from it. Make whatever other changes are necessary.
Example: *Peter behaves like a child.*
Answer: *Peter behaves in a childish way.*

1 With eyes filled with **tears**, she begged him to forgive her.

2 In all **likelihood**, he will come.

3 He shows no **respect** for his elders.

4 He feels nothing but **contempt** for thieves and liars.

5 They **melted** the iron and poured it into special molds.

6 They couldn't **explain** his behaviour.

7 There is no **possibility** of his passing the exam.

8 Both machines and people often **fail**.

Task Two >>> Fill in the blanks with appropriate **PREPOSITIONS**.

1 'Did the manager promise you a raise?' 'Yes, he committed himself _____ it some time ago.'

2 'Is he really as incompetent as they say?'
'Yes, it is his incompetence that has prevented him _____ being promoted.'

3 'Sweden is said to have plenty of raw materials.' 'It abounds _____ them.'

4 'John's car was badly damaged in the accident.' 'Exactly, he may as well write it _____.'

5 'Did you protest about the assistant's rude behavior?'
'Of course, I couldn't pass the matter _____ without protesting.'

6 'Why does he go for brunettes?' 'They appeal _____ him, I think.'

7 'Did Pete join the Navy as he said he would?'
'No, he decided _____ a career in the Army, I think.'

8 'Did he say 'yes' to their demand?'
'To accede _____ such a demand would establish a dangerous precedent.'

36

Task Three >>> Underline the correct word in each parenthesis.

1. Missionaries usually try to (convert - pervert) pagans to Christianity.
2. It's my (convention - conviction) that he is a fraud.
3. Mr. Jones is our baseball (coach - couch).
4. Unfortunately, he (reverted - retorted) to drinking again.
5. I don't like people who are (cross - gross) with me.
6. Contagious diseases are not easy to (localise - locate).
7. When I broke the news to her, she began to (wipe - weep).
8. Eskimos used to travel on (ledges - sledges).
9. The bloodthirsty (mop - mob) wanted revenge.
10. The police have (inclusive - conclusive) evidence as to who committed the murder.

Task Four >>> Fill in the blanks with appropriate PREPOSITIONS.

1. 'Do you like your new English teacher?'   'Yes, I think I have a crush _____ him.'
2. 'Did you take on the new job, eventually?'   'I did, but it calls _____ a lot of work.'
3. 'Do you think Gary is the sort of man to be entrusted with so much money?'
   'Oh yes. He's a man _____ impeccable honesty.'
4. 'He's in complete disagreement with you, isn't he?'
   'Yes, it'll be some time before I bring him _____ to my point of view.'
5. 'What about that clever scheme of yours? Did you pull it off?'   'No, it fell _____ like all the others.'
6. 'What a vicious-looking dog the Browns have got!'
   'Yes, it came _____ me all of a sudden when I passed their house the other day.'
7. 'It's rumored that he is a billionaire!'   'He's not so rich as people make him _____ to be.'
8. 'Can I sleep on this sofa?'   'It is not meant _____ sleeping on, you know.'
9. 'What time did you get home last night?'
   'At three in the morning. The party didn't break _____ before two.'
10. 'I have a complaint to make.'
    'The manager is not available at the moment, madam, but I could look _____ the matter if you like.'

Vocabulary Practice

A. Read the text below and choose the correct word A, B C or D to fit the gaps.

Slavery was not the only **(11)**................................ of life in New Orleans that would have been unfamiliar to men like Captain Amos Stoddard, a New Englander who became one of the **(12)**................................ of the new lands. Stoddard might have been **(13)**................................ by the odd cultural mix that New Orleans represented, and which it still **(14)**................................, in some forms, to this day. After the Spanish ceded Louisiana to the French, much of the Spanish population in New Orleans departed for Cuba. As they left and French immigrants came in from Francophone **(15)**................................ like San Domingue, New Orleans took on a Gallic tinge. At the same time, traces of Spanish occupation remained strong, with luxurious homes in the city built in Spanish style, around courtyards and with stucco walls. As a further **(16)**................................ of the territory's past governments, the Louisiana State Legislature met in the former palace of the Spanish governors, until it burned down in 1827. In what might **(17)**................................ readers today as a particularly chilling reminder of the city's previous masters, two pillories stood on Chartres Street. The Spanish authorities had locked prisoners in those stocks and sometimes publicly humiliated and abused them.

Thomas Jefferson, the American President, in purchasing Louisiana and bringing about the **(18)**................................ of control that occurred on December 20, opened a new **(19)**................................ in American history and closed the old one, of which he had been a principal author. Only a few years before, he had rejected Alexander Hamilton's proposal for a national bank by **(20)**................................ that the Constitution didn't empower the U.S. government to create such an institution. By 1803 he seems to have changed his feelings about the problem of "implied powers" - or at least been excited enough about the possible uses of 828,000 square miles of property to set aside any legal qualms.

11. **A.** aspect	**B.** position	**C.** view	**D.** look
12. **A.** slave traders	**B.** numbers	**C.** governors	**D.** many
13. **A.** interested	**B.** frightened	**C.** perplexed	**D.** humoured
14. **A.** refrains	**B.** retains	**C.** relinquishes	**D.** replaces
15. **A.** continents	**B.** industries	**C.** colonies	**D.** pasts
16. **A.** examination	**B.** reference	**C.** plunder	**D.** reminder
17. **A.** present	**B.** strike	**C.** inspire	**D.** instill
18. **A.** hand-over	**B.** transaction	**C.** ownership	**D.** transfer
19. **A.** chapter	**B.** book	**C.** piece	**D.** paragraph
20. **A.** registering	**B.** arguing	**C.** bickering	**D.** demanding

B. Fill the gaps in the following sentences with the correct answer A, B C or D.

21 It's my _____ that he's a fraud.
   a conviction   **b** choice   **c** indignation   **d** mistrust

22 He _____ hard to make a success of his life.
   a saved   **b** plunged   **c** strove   **d** throve

23 He took no _____ of what I said.
   a advice   **b** revenge   **c** warning   **d** notice

24 Could you possibly _____ me at the next committee meeting?
   a stand in for   **b** make up for   **c** go back on   **d** keep in with

25 Tax _____ deprives the nation or several million dollars a year.
   a retention   **b** evasion   **c** invasion   **d** desertion

26 The minister let it be known that he would sue for _____.
   a praise   **b** diligence   **c** deface   **d** defamation

27 Her derisive remark _____ the crowd.
   a engulfed   **b** engrossed   **c** enlivened   **d** enraged

28 She was so infuriated that she found it difficult to _____ her temper.
   a contain   **b** abstain   **c** retain   **d** detain

29 The theory he put forward concerning the origin of species was highly _____.
   a disgraced   **b** discredited   **c** debased   **d** dishonored

30 Hostile rivalry often involves defaming one's _____.
   a friends   **b** relatives   **c** colleagues   **d** opponents

Unit 10

Words in Action

Exercise A >>> Match the definitions of occupations below with the words in the box.

playwright milliner plumber locksmith potter thatcher   hardware dealer   peddler fishmonger cobbler

1. A wandering merchant selling small wares is a hawker or a(n) _____.
2. A man who works as a shoemaker mending and patching shoes is a(n) _____.
3. A man who makes earthen-ware is a(n) _____.
4. A writer of plays is a(n) _____.
5. A person employed in making, trimming or selling bonnets, men's hats, etc is a(n) _____.
6. Someone who works in a shop that sells fish is a(n) _____.
7. A maker or repairer of locks is a(n) _____.
8. A person whose job is to connect or repair water and drainage pipes, baths, toilets etc. is a(n) _____.
9. A person who makes roofs of houses with straw or reeds is a(n) _____.
10. A shopkeeper who sells hardware, especially metal goods, is a(n) _____.

Exercise B >>> Match each of the following definitions with a word from the box.
Example: *A young person who commits minor crimes or vandalism and who is not old enough yet to be legally considered an adult is a (juvenile)* **delinquent**.

| mugger   poacher   assassin   perjurer   usurper   stowaway   trespasser |
hijacker   hobo   hooligan   quack   usurer   vagrant   tax-evader   forger

1. Someone who catches or shoots animals, birds or fish on private land unlawfully and without permission is a(n) _____.
2. Someone who alters a genuine piece of writing especially somebody else's signature in order to deceive is a(n) _____.
3. A man who attacks another usually from behind with the intention of robbing him is a(n) _____.
4. Someone who murders by assault, especially a public or eminent person, usually for political motives, is a(n) _____.
5. Someone who lends money at an exorbitant rate which is illegal is a(n) _____.
6. Someone who forcibly seizes (kingly) power is a(n) _____.
7. Someone who gives false testimony before a court of law while under oath is a(n) _____.
8. Someone who does not pay the full amount of tax that he should is a(n) _____.
9. One who hides on a vessel in order to obtain free passage without paying a fare is a(n) _____.
10. A person without a settled home who wanders aimlessly from place to place, begging or stealing in order to live is a(n) _____.
11. A tramp or a vagrant who has no regular work or home, especially one who travels from place to place and gets money by begging is a(n) _____.
12. One who pretends to possess medical knowledge especially in the field of salves that is, ointments for local ailments, is a(n) _____.
13. One of a gang of disorderly and noisy persons behaving in a violent and destructive way is a(n) _____.
14. One who seizes control of an aircraft while in flight by the threat or use of force and directs it to a different destination is a(n) _____.
15. One who violates privately owned land without right or permission is a(n) _____.

Exercise C >>> Match each of the following definitions with a word from the box.
Example: *A large number of bees flying together is a swarm of bees.*

| pack   shoal/school   constellation   congregation   band   squad   mob |
| conglomeration   cluster/clump   sheaf   heap   pile |

1 A large number of fish swimming together _____
2 A group of church attendees _____
3 A group of different people or things _____
4 A number of trees, bushes, etc growing close together _____
5 A quantity of things placed neatly one on top of the other _____
6 A quantity of things in a rather untidy arrangement _____
7 A bundle of papers or corn tied together _____
8 A disorderly crowd of people _____
9 A small group of policemen who form a unit or a section of a police force that is responsible for dealing with a particular type of crime _____
10 A group of bandits under a leader _____
11 A group of fixed stars in the sky forming a pattern _____
12 A group of animals, especially wolves or dogs hunting together _____

Exercise D >>> Read the text below and choose the correct word a, b, c or d to fit the gaps.

The current emphasis on language as a social phenomenon will open the way to ____(1) communicative language-learning approaches at all school levels. The focus on the social purposes of language will ____(2) that interaction among persons in a society and ____(3) societies will become more harmonious and more significant ____(4) the use of clear but polite language in ____(5) the native and the second language is taught and practised in schools in meaningful and interesting social situations.

1 a widespread
   b wide-known
   c wide-awake
   d wide open

2 a assure
   b reassure
   c insure
   d ensure

3 a along
   b across
   c above
   d over

4 a as
   b so
   c by
   d why

5 a either
   b both
   c neither
   d none

41

Vocabulary Practice

A. Read the text below and choose the correct word A, B C or D to fit the gaps.

Many separate fires **(11)**........................... in the humus of the forest floor. Smoke sometimes **12)**...........................
the sun, which was often visible only at midday. On September 30, flames came within three miles of the town of Green Bay, **(13)**........................... 1,200 cords of wood stored at a charcoal kiln.

The settlements in the area were becoming increasingly **(14)**........................... from both the outside world and one another as railroad and telegraph lines burned. The fires seemed to wax and wane, **(15)**...........................on the wind and chance. On September 30 the Marinette and Peshtigo Eagle reported hopefully that "the fires have nearly **(16)**........................... now in this vicinity."

But the paper was wrong, and the fires were growing. By October 4, the smoke was so thick on Green Bay that ships had to use their foghorns and **(17)**........................... by compass. On October 7, the paper, reduced to looking for any scrap of good news, noted that at least the smoke had greatly reduced the mosquito population and that "a certain establishment down on the bay shore that has been **(18)**........................... to the respectable citizens" had burned.

The paper's editor, **(19)**........................... by the burning of the telegraph line, could not know it, but a large, deep low-pressure area was moving in from the west. The winds circling it would turn the smoldering forest of northeastern Wisconsin into **(20)**........................... on earth.

11. **A.** extinguished	**B.** engulfed	**C.** spread	**D.** smoldered
12. **A.** obscured	**B.** burnt	**C.** illuminated	**D.** exposed
13. **A.** damaging	**B.** consuming	**C.** avoiding	**D.** licking
14. **A.** frightened	**B.** lonely	**C.** isolated	**D.** inundated
15. **A.** depending	**B.** independent	**C.** waiting	**D.** from
16. **A.** increased	**B.** died out	**C.** flared	**D.** diminished
17. **A.** steer	**B.** drive	**C.** guess	**D.** navigate
18. **A.** frequented	**B.** obnoxious	**C.** open	**D.** ignorant
19. **A.** cut-off	**B.** burnt	**C.** dismissed	**D.** chased
20. **A.** peace	**B.** heaven	**C.** hell	**D.** paradise

B. Fill the gaps in the following sentences with the correct answer A, B C or D.

21 Good use of language _____ its beauty and development.
    a detracts from   **b** deteriorates   **c** enhances   **d** lessens

22 Complete the form as _____ in the notes below.
    a insisted   **b** specified   **c** implied   **d** devised

23 He shuns work as he is such a(n) _____ student.
    a indolent   **b** diligent   **c** indigent   **d** indigenous

24 The student's grammar was _____.
    a well-constructed   **b** incoherent   **c** jerry-built   **d** highbrow

25 His spelling was _____.
    a ferocious   **b** incongruous   **c** apprehensive   **d** atrocious

26 The notice on the villa gate read: '_____ will be prosecuted'.
    a Muggers   **b** Hijackers   **c** Stowaways   **d** Trespassers

27 He lied under oath in court and was subsequently charged with _____.
    a poaching   **b** forgery   **c** perjury   **d** usury

28 Not only is little Johnny's grammar incoherent and his spelling atrocious but also his punctuation _____.
    a slothful   **b** sluggish   **c** hazard   **d** haphazard

29 I'm not a habitual smoker, but I occasionally _____ in a cigarette.
    a enjoy   **b** indulge   **c** divulge   **d** decline

30 We could discern a _____ of cottages in the distance.
    a constellation   **b** clutter   **c** cluster   **d** piled

Unit 11

Words in Action

All of the following verbs denote a sense of **giving up**. Study their definitions carefully and then use the words to fill in the blanks in the sentences on the next page. In some sentences, more than one verb may be appropriate.

abandon leave or withdraw completely and forever; give up or bring to an end
  e.g. *He abandoned his wrecked car on the freeway.*

forsake (forsook-forsaken) desert; leave forever; give up completely
  e.g. *He forsook his fortune to devote himself to the church.*

  (a man may *abandon* his home or *forsake* his friends)

abdicate give up officially (an official position, esp. that of king or queen)

resign give up (a job or position)
  e.g. *A monarch abdicates while an employee resigns.*

quit stop doing something and leave
  e.g. *He quit his job and went abroad.* (quit is used informally)

surrender give up or give in to power (esp. of an enemy), as a sign of defeat
  e.g. *After days of fighting, the enemy finally surrendered.*

cede give (usually land or a right) to another country or person, esp. after losing a war
  e.g. *The Louisiana colony was ceded to Spain in 1762.*

desert (esp. of military service) leave without authority or permission
  e.g. *A soldier who deserts from the army is severely punished.*

relinquish give up (power, position, a claim, etc.)
  e.g. *One can relinquish a claim, hope or privilege, etc.*

discard (of something useless or unwanted) throw away or put aside
  e.g. *Don't discard your train ticket before you reach your destination.*

evacuate take all the people away from (a place); move (a person) away from a place in order to protect them from danger
  e.g. *The defeated army was forced to evacuate the conquered territory.*

renounce give up (a claim); say formally that one does not own or has no more connection with
  e.g. *He renounced his religion and became a Christian.*

yield give up control of (surrender) to superior forces
  e.g. *A politician may yield to public pressure and an army may yield their position to the enemy.*

Exercise A >>> Fill in the blanks with the suitable verb.

1 It would be most unwise to _____ the map which shows the route before we reach our destination.
2 The inconsiderate husband took to drinking and soon _____ his wife and child.
3 The cowardly soldier was court-marshaled for _____ his post.
4 As a result of the earthquake, the panic-stricken people _____ their homes leaving all their belongings behind.
5 The president was most unwilling to _____ his privileges.
6 When the man went bankrupt, all his friends _____ him.
7 On the one hand, I'm not satisfied with my job, on the other hand, I can't _____. It won't be easy to find another one.
8 Shortly after the revolution had broken out, the king found himself obliged to _____.
9 Our troops were forced to _____ when they were overwhelmed by superior enemy forces.
10 Mr. Rankine decided to _____ when he was passed over in favor of young Brown.
11 The besieged people vowed to die in battle rather than _____ their national territory to the invading army.
12 Mr. Smith is a very indulgent father. He always _____ to his son's wishes.
13 The early Christians, who didn't _____ their faith in Christianity, usually formed a part of the spectacle in the Colosseum.
14 When you wash the lettuce, you should _____ the outside leaves first.
15 Governments don't usually _____ to pressure from the opposition, but from the public.

Exercise B >>> Read the text below and choose the correct word A, B C or D to fit the gaps.

The impact of the Great Depression on Europe was as memorable and decisive in its way as the French Revolution or the First World War. The ____(1) of the Depression can be precisely dated.

American stock markets had prospered almost uninterruptedly since 1921 and had grown fantastically for eighteen months. On 24th, October 1929, the ____(2) halted; share prices fell even faster than they had risen, and thousands of ____(3) were ruined. The American financial crash soon hit Europe.

American loans to Europe had already stopped; now American purchases from Europe stopped also. The European economy was ____(4) balanced. Recovery had brought a great increase in productive powers, with little corresponding increase in markets. ____(5) had also been maintained by the flood of American dollars. Now European factories, too, closed their gates. Within two years, world trade was more than halved. Unemployment soared, particularly in the more industrialised countries. There were over two million unemployed in Great Britain and six million in Germany.

1 a onset
   b outset
   c offset
   d onslaught

2 a boom
   b boon
   c bonus
   d boor

3 a adventurers
   b hawkers
   c executives
   d speculators

4 a cautiously
   b precautionary
   c precariously
   d precociously

5 a Destitution
   b Prosperity
   c Dereliction
   d Expenditure

Vocabulary Development

Task One >>> The words in the box form the opposites of the words in heavy type in the sentences that follow.
Try to fit the appropriate antonym in each blank.
Example: *Offspring are one's children as opposed to one's parents.*

> obsolete haughty extrovert ameliorate inhale sanity assets
> obscure indolent acquittal abundance prodigal ancestor

1 A **descendant** is a person that is descended from an individual that lived a long time ago as opposed to an _____.

2 To **exhale** is to breathe out air as opposed to _____.

3 To **deteriorate** is to become worse as opposed to _____.

4 A **modern** teaching method is usually new and involves the latest developments as opposed to _____.

5 **Liabilities** are the sums of money owed or debts that must be paid from one company to another as opposed to _____.

6 A **well-known** writer is known far and wide as opposed to _____.

7 **Madness** is an illness of the mind that causes a person to behave in an abnormal way as opposed to _____.

8 An **affable** person is polite and pleasant to others as opposed to _____.

9 An **economical** person spends his money carefully, sensibly, and without waste as opposed to _____.

10 An **introvert** keeps to himself; he is withdrawn rather than spending time with others as opposed to a(n) _____.

11 **Conviction** is the decision of a court of law that finds somebody guilty as opposed to _____.

12 A **diligent** student is habitually and constantly hardworking as opposed to _____.

13 **Scarcity** denotes a state of not being plentiful so that something is not easy to find as opposed to _____.

Task Two >>>

Rewrite the following sentences by removing the **ADVERB** in heavy type and substituting it with the **adjective** derived from the adverb. Make any other changes you think necessary.
*Example: How can I **possibly** sleep in a tiny place like this?*
Answer: *How is it possible for me to sleep in a tiny place like this?*

1 What he said sounded **utterly** nonsensical.

2 They were **abjectly** poor.

3 He was **absurdly** demanding.

4 'Can I fly **directly** from Rome to Toronto?' he inquired.

5 That's what his father **actually** said.

6 It's **generally** assumed that money brings happiness.

7 We were **heartily** welcomed by the villagers.

8 The English **avidly** read newspapers and magazines.

9 People think **highly** of him.

Task Three >>>

Tick which answer is closest in meaning to the word or phrase in heavy type.

1 In my opinion, he is not versatile **as regards** teaching. ☐ with reference to ☐ irrespective of
2 I'm afraid I'm **at odds** with my boss. ☐ in agreement ☐ in disagreement
3 He was so persuasive that **I caved in to** his argument. ☐ defended ☐ gave in to
4 My son invariably **turns a deaf ear** to my advice. ☐ follows ☐ pays no heed
5 I'm never **at ease** before an interview. ☐ I'm always ill at ease ☐ I always stand at ease
6 He **has the edge** on you. ☐ he's worse than ☐ he's better than
7 Let's **wind up** the evening with a drink. ☐ start ☐ finish
8 His lecture was **long-winded**. ☐ lengthy and tedious ☐ brief and to the point
9 The speaker held his audience **spell-bound**. ☐ by force ☐ with their attention held as if by magic
10 He's **down in the dumps** again! ☐ he works down in the pits ☐ he feels depressed and miserable

Task One >>>

Rewrite the following sentences beginning with the word(s) in heavy type. Make whatever changes are necessary.

Example: *They made **Peter** empty his pockets.* **Answer:** *Peter was made to empty his pockets.*

1 How difficult it is for a young poet **to earn** his living.

2 They presented a medal to **each of the lifeboatmen**.

3 He couldn't possibly have found **any other** occupation to suit his needs so well.

4 The trade unions were blamed for **all the trouble**.

5 It might have been a pleasant outing if we **had** set out earlier.

6 It is specifically **this kind of task** from which we are exempted.

7 They found that **30% of the population** was suffering from malnutrition.

8 A man's real influence is exerted **only** after his death.

9 We, in the U.S., are at present in the middle of **an influenza epidemic**.

10 Continued research on modern science may lead to **a fearful destruction** of the environment.

11 You must deal with **this problem** at greater length.

12 It is more difficult to answer his question than **yours**.

Task Two >>> Tick the one word or phrase that is closest in meaning to the word(s) in heavy type.

1 Three of them **bit the dust** during the shoot out.   ☐ got dusty   ☐ were killed
2 What he said put me **in a spot**.   ☐ in a difficult position   ☐ in a dilemma
3 He'll **blow his top** if he finds out what you've done.   ☐ be angry   ☐ be sad
4 He **came within an ace of** being run over.   ☐ he had a narrow escape   ☐ he holds all the aces
5 Most of the visitors here are predominantly of north European **stock**.   ☐ mentality   ☐ ancestry
6 I have to **sweat my guts out** to make a living.   ☐ work very hard   ☐ loiter about
7 'Is he a good teacher?' '**Not by a long shot**.'   ☐ not at all   ☐ so so
8 It's no use talking to me about metaphysics. **It's a closed book to me**.   ☐ It is forbidden   ☐ I don't know anything about it
9 He's **round the bend**.   ☐ reasonable   ☐ insane
10 I'm **on edge** about this new play I'm putting on.   ☐ tense and nervous   ☐ busy and worried

Task Three >>> In each of the following sentences, replace the words in heavy type with a single word from the box with the same meaning.
Example: *I judged from the state of the sky that a thunderstorm was **coming shortly** (imminent).*

| carcass | avarice | extortion | incapacitated | pageantry | impunity | replica |
| impartiality | decapitation | mob | piety | perjury | amenities | alimony | armistice |

1 **Obtaining money by using threats and violence** _____ is an offense punishable by law.
2 **The dead body** _____ of the deer was torn to pieces by the jackals.
3 The judge is known for his **unbiased and fair judgment**. _____
4 You can't disregard the law with **freedom from punishment**. _____
5 He missed the **agreeable features and facilities** _____ of the city.
6 England is rich in **old traditions and customs preserved among the common people**. _____
7 She lives on the **allowance by order of court** _____ from her former husband.
8 He was charged with **giving false testimony to a court while under oath**. _____
9 The model was a **reproduction in exact detail** _____ of his own yacht.
10 **Greed for amassing riches** _____ is a vice.
11 The **uncontrolled and disorderly crowd of people** _____ committed outrages.
12 In many people's opinion, an **agreement made during a war that would stop hostilities for a limited period of time** _____ would be an act of high treason.
13 He was **unable to work** _____ after the accident.
14 He was punished by **having his head cut off**. _____
15 They were men of **true and deep respect for God**. _____

53

Vocabulary Practice

A. Read the text below and choose the correct word A, B C or D to fit the gaps.

The Depression didn't end until the production (11)................... of World War II, but Franklin Roosevelt's New Deal programs (12)................... to help. One, the Securities and Exchange Commission, was created in 1934 to shift the job of (13)................... securities trade from the states to the federal government. Today brokers and dealers must (14)................... with the SEC, to prevent price manipulation, and there are strict (15)................... for the minimum down payments to buy stocks. Of course although we haven't since experienced a depression on the (16)................... of the one in the 1930s, the SEC hasn't rendered the stock market crash extinct. On October 19, 1987, the Dow suffered its largest one-day (17)................... since 1914, and on April 14, 2000, it fell 617.78 points, the largest-ever single-day point loss.

"I used to be quite an (18)...................," the economist John Kenneth Galbraith once said. "I thought that by keeping the memory of the 1929 crash alive we would have a (19)................... against the kind of feckless, fatuous optimism which caused people to get in and shove up the markets .... and get (20)................... by the illusion of ever-increasing wealth. I've given up on that hope because we've had it happen too often again since."

11. **A.** purge	**B.** end	**C.** demise	**D.** surge
12. **A.** asked	**B.** aimed	**C.** suspected	**D.** failed
13. **A.** ruling	**B.** freeing	**C.** regulating	**D.** demanding
14. **A.** join	**B.** announce	**C.** ally	**D.** register
15. **A.** requirements	**B.** wishes	**C.** laws	**D.** expectations
16. **A.** range	**B.** climb	**C.** scale	**D.** ascend
17. **A.** increase	**B.** collapse	**C.** ferocity	**D.** fall
18. **A.** optimist	**B.** egocentric	**C.** illusionist	**D.** pessimist
19. **A.** knowledge	**B.** warning	**C.** radar	**D.** speculation
20. **A.** carried away	**B.** enthusiastic	**C.** swept	**D.** obscured

B. Fill the gaps in the following sentences with the correct answer A, B C or D.

21 The police _____ the district for the thief.
  a scoured   **b** brushed   **c** ran   **d** penetrated

22 At the _____ moment, he backed out.
  a insignificant   **b** meaningful   **c** crucial   **d** trifling

23 Her house was _____ at a high value.
  a considered   **b** deemed   **c** assessed   **d** appreciated

24 What a(n) _____ appearance he's got!
  a huge   **b** enormous   **c** weird   **d** benevolent

25 Don't be _____ to your elders.
  a affable   **b** consistent   **c** impertinent   **d** respectable

26 He's one of the best doctors in town and held in high _____.
  a esteem   **b** estimation   **c** value   **d** appraisal

27 You may make any changes to the original plan you _____ necessary.
  a evaluate   **b** recommend   **c** esteem   **d** deem

28 I've got something of great importance to _____ to you.
  a impair   **b** compare   **c** impart   **d** deport

29 Too many trees round a house _____ it of air and light.
  a deprive   **b** deprave   **c** deride   **d** derive

30 The bloodthirsty _____ wanted to avenge their leader's death.
  a mop   **b** mob   **c** clog   **d** flog

54

Unit 13

Words in Action

> plague - conflagration - deluge - drought - landslide - earthquake - famine - destitution
> avalanche - insanity - contamination - depression - subsidence - holocaust - gale

Exercise A >>> The following definitions refer to the words above. They all have **unpleasant connotations** as they are related to disasters, calamities, bad living conditions, natural phenomena, etc. Study them carefully, and then fill each blank with the word that corresponds to its definition.

1 A wide-spread scarcity or dearth of food that causes people to suffer from extreme hunger. _____

2 An unusually great flood accompanied by heavy rainfall that causes inundation such as that which affected Noah and his ark. _____

3 A long continuous spell of dry weather with marked lack of rain that stems the growth of plants. _____

4 Extreme poverty often accompanied by lack of property. _____

5 The sinking of the earth to a lower level because of underground movements and workings. _____

6 A strong and violent wind but of less force than that of a storm or tempest. _____

7 A very large scale destruction and loss of life that may result from use of strategic weapons, as in a nuclear war. _____

8 The slipping of a mass of land from a higher to a lower level. _____

9 An extremely contagious pestilence or epidemic disease, also known as the Black Death, that decimated Europe's population in the Middle Ages. _____

10 A decline in business marked by an extreme slump in production and purchase of foods such as the Great Crash on Wall Street in 1929, which ruined international trade. _____

11 A condition or state where the environment (water, air, soil) is made impure because of harmful chemicals and poisonous matter. _____

12 The fall of a mass of snow or ice down a mountain slope. _____

13 A great or disastrous fire, especially one breaking out in a forest. _____

14 A vibration of the earth's crust caused by disturbances of the inner layers of the earth. _____

15 Any mental disorder characterized by irrational or violent deviation from normal thinking. _____

Vocabulary Practice

A. Read the text below and choose the correct word A, B C or D to fit the gaps.

Detroit **(11)**.....................St. Patrick's Day in Corktown, a neighborhood named for the many **(12)**.....................
workers from County Cork. Some of the original workers' row houses there are being **(13)**....................., and the
area is listed on the National Register of Historic Places. The parade covers about a dozen blocks along Michigan
Avenue, on Sunday, March 12.
  The March 12 parade in San Francisco begins at 11:30 a.m. at Second and Market Streets and
(14)..................... to the Civic Center Plaza. San Francisco's first celebration, in 1851, **(15)**..................... of a
small party in Hayes Valley and a Shamrock Ball at a saloon on Pacific Street. Enthusiasm for the holiday waxed and
waned over the years, but by 1956 it had become **(16)**....................., with 35,000 marchers.
San Diego **(17)**..................... its twenty-sixth St. Patrick's Day parade on Saturday, March 11, at 11 a.m. Glittery
Las Vegas, Nevada, will have its fortieth one on Saturday, March 18, at 11 a.m. To the south, the Irish in Tucson,
Arizona, will step out at the same time.
  (18)..................... in bathing suits usually line the parade route in the Waikiki Beach district of Honolulu.
(19)..................... to Pat Bigold, a writer who is half Irish, his city's St. Patrick's Day celebration on March 17 is
the closest to the international **(20)**..................... . It takes place at noon, which is 5 p.m. in Boston.

11. **A.** commemorates	**B.** commiserates	**C.** celebrates	**D.** participates
12. **A.** immigrant	**B.** vagrant	**C.** destitute	**D.** hard
13. **A.** kept	**B.** flooded	**C.** demolished	**D.** preserved
14. **A.** detours	**B.** diverts	**C.** heads	**D.** retreats
15. **A.** was	**B.** consisted	**C.** devised	**D.** contrived
16. **A.** common	**B.** unpopular	**C.** localised	**D.** mainstream
17. **A.** kicks off	**B.** forwards	**C.** redirects	**D.** hands over
18. **A.** Audience	**B.** Addressers	**C.** Listeners	**D.** Spectators
19. **A.** According	**B.** Assuming	**C.** Listening	**D.** Deliberating
20. **A.** border	**B.** code	**C.** dateline	**D.** season

B. Fill the gaps in the following sentences with the correct answer A, B C or D.

21 The ship's masts were all destroyed in the strong _____.
  a gales   **b** deluge   **c** famine   **d** eruption

22 They were, superficially at any _____, a very unlikely pair to become friends.
  a aspect   **b** chance   **c** extent   **d** rate

23 The kidnapper had tried to _____ her before.
  a speculate   **b** abduct   **c** dispel   **d** infer

24 He's a very _____ writer whom few people have ever heard of.
  a wrinkled   **b** congested   **c** pale   **d** obscure

25 His untimely death _____ the decline of the empire.
  a shrank   **b** ameliorated   **c** precipitated   **d** exaggerated

26 David was given all the _____ for rescuing the drowning boy.
  a merit   **b** blame   **c** credit   **d** reputation

27 Empires are born, they _____ and finally fall into decline.
  a profit   **b** culminate   **c** deviate   **d** convert

28 During the _____, he was afraid none of his family would survive.
  a famine   **b** destitution   **c** subsidy   **d** eloquence

29 The whole forest area was devastated by _____.
  a plague   **b** famine   **c** insanity   **d** conflagration

30 Hedgehogs, bears and other animals that hibernate remain _____ during winter.
  a superficial   **b** passive   **c** dormitory   **d** dormant

Unit 14

Words in Action

wet	covered with liquid	drenched	made wet all over
moist	slightly wet	sodden	filled with water, heavy with wetness
damp	rather wet in an unpleasant way	muggy	(of weather) unpleasantly warm, not dry, almost sticky
humid	(of weather) having a lot of wetness in the air and usually very hot	sultry	(of weather) airless and oppressive
soaked	thoroughly wet		
saturated	so wet that no more water can be absorbed		
soggy	unpleasantly filled or covered with water so that there is lack of firmness		

NOTE: If you are caught in a downpour without an umbrella, you become either **soaked, drenched to the skin, dripping wet** or **saturated**. If it is cold as well, you may be **frozen to the bone** or **chilled to the marrow**.

Exercise A >>> Fill in the blanks in the following sentences with the appropriate word from the words in the parentheses.

1 Don't sit on that bench, the paint is still _____. **(wet, saturated)**

2 It was so hot and _____ that day that we decided not to go on a picnic. **(humid, soggy)**

3 He looked innocent, and his eyes were huge and _____ with tears. **(sodden, moist)**

4 It is during the rainy season in West Africa, when it is hot and humid, and people feel sticky and tired, that we speak of _____ weather. **(soaked, muggy)**

5 To wipe a window, we normally use a _____ piece of cloth. **(soggy, damp)**

6 It began pouring with rain, and all the summer hikers got _____. **(humid, drenched)**

7 It was fortunate that we had taken a pair of blankets with us, which we spread onto the _____ ground before we sat down to rest our aching feet. **(damp, muggy)**

8 When playgrounds are provided with water, children are fond of getting _____. **(saturated, wet)**

9 In underground places such as cellars and caves, the air is dank and _____. **(damp, soaked)**

10 After working in the field for several hours, Joseph was _____ with sweat. **(muggy, drenched)**

Exercise B >>> All the verbs in the following sentences are used with a meaning different from their original one. Replace all the verbs in heavy type with another verb or phrase to show that you understand the way they're used.   **Example:** *The Queen's son was **created** Prince of Wales (appointed)*

1 He's a man of esteem who **commands** respect. _____

2 All the people in the village **observed** the traditions handed down to them by their ancestors. _____

3 The car **gathered** speed and was soon lost from sight. _____

4 The house will **fetch** at least £270,000. _____

5 We were overwhelmed by the hearty welcome they **extended** to us. _____

6 It's absurd to **entertain** such a foolish idea. _____

7 The manager flatly refused to **commit himself**. _____

8 The medicine should be **administered** according to the prescription. _____

9 We would like to **advise** you that your account with us has been overdrawn since May 6th. _____

10 The bank refused to **back** their plan. _____

Vocabulary Practice

A. Read the text below and choose the correct word A, B C or D to fit the gaps.

Now, nearly 40 years later, the Cold War is over, but Churchill's ideals - **(11)**..................., democracy, freedom - are just as relevant. So Westminster decided to give its galleries "on the lion of the twentieth century" a twenty-first-century **(12)**.................... . In the museum's new permanent collection, multimedia **(13)**.................... trace Churchill's life, philosophy, and writing, concentrating heavily on World War II and the "Sinews of Peace" speech; a "leadership corridor" compares him with other British and American **(14)**.................... . The rededication **(15)**.................... tonight with a talk by Churchill's daughter and granddaughter and continues over the weekend with a community luncheon, black-tie gala, and a keynote address by the TV news **(16)**.................... Chris Matthews.

Another exhibit, **(17)**.................... to the Cold War itself, shows how true Churchill's predictions proved to be. Of course his **(18)**.................... was a long time coming. When he arrived in Richmond three days after his Westminster speech to address the Virginia General Assembly, he **(19)**.................... the controversy he had created. "You have not asked to see beforehand what I am going to say," he remarked to the legislators. "I might easily **(20)**.................... a lot of things people know in their hearts are true but are a bit shy of saying in public."

11. **A.** persistence **B.** vigilance **C.** power **D.** fussiness
12. **A.** refresh **B.** instigation **C.** update **D.** renew
13. **A.** exhibits **B.** demonstrations **C.** evidence **D.** gadgets
14. **A.** governments **B.** politics **C.** tyrants **D.** rulers
15. **A.** is **B.** kicks off **C.** ends **D.** continues
16. **A.** celebrity **B.** mogul **C.** anchor **D.** hot shot
17. **A.** geared **B.** denouncing **C.** commiserating **D.** dedicated
18. **A.** vindication **B.** conviction **C.** prediction **D.** pessimism
19. **A.** accepted **B.** declined **C.** acknowledged **D.** greeted
20. **A.** conceal **B.** blurt-out **C.** lie about **D.** assume

B. Fill the gaps in the following sentences with the correct answer A, B C or D.

21 We had to _____ to get through the low doorway.
 a bow **b** shrug **c** stoop **d** kneel

22 When the company closed down because of financial difficulties, I was made _____.
 a frivolous **b** surplus **c** disabled **d** redundant

23 Our journey through China was _____ with difficulties.
 a beset **b** surrounded **c** assaulted **d** devoid

24 It was teeming down with rain and we all got _____.
 a dripping **b** humid **c** damp **d** soaked

25 Mary, you look _____ today.
 a promoted **b** modified **c** gorgeous **d** avid

26 God is _____.
 a omnivorous **b** omnipotent **c** herbivorous **d** carnivorous

27 It was so hot and _____ that day that we couldn't possibly have gone for an outing.
 a moist **b** sultry **c** frozen **d** soggy

28 She didn't realize at that time how dull and _____ her life had been.
 a dreary **b** enchanting **c** engrossed **d** exciting

29 It's absurd to _____ such a foolish idea.
 a extend **b** entertain **c** administer **d** commit

30 Experts will _____ IQ tests among school-goers and quote the results.
 a promote **b** take **c** administer **d** complete

Unit 15

Words in Action

Exercise A >>> Match the words in the box with their antonyms below.

A conclusive	B incurable	C in the pink	D out of the blue	E boisterous
F advocate	G indolent	H propensity	I illiteracy	J pious

1 active _____ 2 aversion _____ 3 expectedly _____ 4 oppose _____ 5 ill _____
6 docile _____ 7 atheistic _____ 8 inconclusive _____ 9 curable _____ 10 literacy _____

Exercise B >>> Now, fill in the blanks using the words above.

1 His essay paper was based on the widespread _____ in Asia.
2 The defendant was acquitted due to _____ evidence.
3 Scott, who was supposed to be in New York, seemed to arrive _____.
4 Well, Mrs. Jones, you certainly look _____ since you returned from your holiday.
5 The children were as _____ as lambs.
6 As we approach the 21st century, it seems that more _____ diseases are cropping up than ever before.
7 There was a _____ crowd waiting to see the basketball hero, Michael Jordan.
8 I don't know if I'm the cause, but it seems as though he has a natural _____ to argue.
9 He is said to have been a _____ man who served his church dutifully.
10 In both World Wars, the United States _____ Germany.

61

Vocabulary Development

Task One >>> Rephrase the following sentences so that each new sentence contains a **DERIVATIVE** of the word in heavy type.

Example: *In 1975, the country obtained its* **independence**.
Answer: *In 1975, the country became <u>independent</u>.*

1. In 1975, New Guinea became a **sovereign** state.
   In 1975, Australia was forced to give up _____ over the island.
2. It's a nation **diverse** in ethnic elements. It's a nation marked by ethnic _____.
3. We were enchanted by their **spontaneous** welcome.
   We were enchanted by the _____ of their welcome.
4. Timbering has **devastated** the countryside.
   The _____ of the countryside is ascribed to timbering.
5. Villagers are **superstitious**. Villagers are filled with _____.
6. They **believe** in spirits. They have a strong _____ in spirits.
7. Some villagers are **sorcerers**. Some villagers practice _____.
8. Sir Lokoloko **reconfirmed** the national philosophy.
   A _____ of the national philosophy was given by Sir Lokoloko.
9. The people are **poor**. The people live in _____.
10. They suffer from **malnutrition**. They are _____.
11. It is a country of high **illiteracy**. It is a country with a high percentage of _____ people.
12. A lot of people appeared to be **hungry** and **ill**.
    A lot of people appeared to be suffering from _____ and _____.
13. New Guinea strikes you as a **sparsely** populated country.
    The _____ of population in New Guinea is striking.
14. The people are **pious, hard-working** and above all **naive**.
    The people are marked by _____ _____, and above all _____.
15. Most areas on the **coast** are covered with swamps.
    Most _____ areas are covered with swamps.
16. They put all their efforts into **prestige** projects.
    The projects they put all their efforts into are _____.

Task Two >>> In the sentences below, you are given the first two letters of a verb ending in **-ate** Complete the verbs based on the definition given in the sentence printed before it.
Example: Things that occur after each other or follow in turns.
   His life al____ between work and sleep. (Answer: alternates).

1. To put an end to something.
   The chairman te_____ the discussion by calling the members to vote on the proposed motion.
2. To start to find the origin of something.
   The dispute over the sovereignty of the island or_____ in the hatred between the two neighboring countries.
3. To give people an injection, called a vaccine, to protect them from disease caused by germs.
   The doctor va_____ all the members of the local tribe against contagious diseases.

4 To be powerful, important and have control over people or things.

   Once Europe do_____ over the rest of the world by colonising many parts of it.

5 To choose someone thought suitable for a job and appoint him to office.

   The Prime Minister no_____ a committee to investigate the charges brought against his finance ministers by the opposition.

6 To get rid of something by removing it completely.

   In a welfare state poverty should be el_____.

7 To organize the efforts of the people taking part in a project and put their activities into proper relation.

   Productivity can be increased if we co_____ organization with hard work.

8 To contribute or give money to a charity without asking for anything in return.

   Mrs. Thomas do_____ £1000 to the children's hospital.

9 To give an area a particular description so that a function is either allowed or not to occur in it.

   Smoking is prohibited in the non-smoking de_____ areas.

10 To want to feel young and vigorous again.

   Many a woman cherishes the illusion that cosmetics can re_____ her.

Task Three >>>

In each of the following sentences, the word in heavy type is incorrect. Write the correct word which is similar in form to the word in heavy type.

Example: *The Reverend Doubledock preaches here on **alternative** Sundays.*
Answer: *alternate*

SENTENCE WITH MISTAKES — CORRECT WORDS

1 The notion you put forward will be discussed at a **consequent** meeting.

2 He came to **canvas** my vote in the forthcoming election.

3 I wouldn't like to transact business with such an **insoluble** company.

4 Young people of an **impressive** age can easily be manipulated.

5 We are always given **preferable** treatment in this hotel.

6 Postponement of their raises and threatened redundancies were the striker's main **griefs**.

7 I can't possibly eat this food; it's **indelible**.

8 It is enjoyable to play to such an **appreciable** audience.

9 He is **illegible** for the post.

10 He was very anxious to learn something of the **contagious** countries.

11 His book was based on **imaginable** incidents and characters.

12 Unfortunately, many wildlife species are now **virtuously** extinct.

13 An **informative** denounced him to the authorities.

14 A friend that can be depended on or trusted is **dependent**.

15 Lower income tax on overtime earnings might act as a **stimulant** to industry.

63

Vocabulary Practice

A. Read the text below and choose the correct word A, B C or D to fit the gaps.

Gambling was legalised in Nevada in 1931 to increase **(11)**............... for the state. Today the casinos are very important for the financial growth of Las Vegas. Bugsy Siegel, the gangster and casino owner, is the **(12)**............... we remember most. A Capone syndicate boss, Siegel came to Las Vegas in the late 1930s and saw a potential gold mine in the book operations that casinos used to take bets on horse races in Florida, New York, and California. Offering his syndicate's race-reporting Continental Wire Service to the bookies at a lower price than any of the existing services, Siegel **(13)**............... the market. Then, in 1942, having **(14)**............... the competition, Siegel abruptly raised the prices and demanded a profit share from each book. Without another source for race results, and frightened by Siegel's connections to Capone, the casinos **(15)**............... .

With the profits, Siegel started his own casino. The ambitious *Flamingo Hotel* was finished in 1946. **(16)**............... on a strip of land along the Los Angeles Highway and designed to be an elegant resort rather than a faux Western gambling hall, the Flamingo forever moved the focus of Las Vegas away from downtown. It also **(17)**............... the success of gambling as the town's major industry. Freed from the **(18)**............... of their Western heritage, European-style casinos and resorts **(19)**............... in the years after 1946. Siegel was shot in a gangland execution in 1947, but his **(20)**............... lives on in the gaudy formalism of casinos like *Caesar's Palace* and *The Sands*.

11. **A.** insurance **B.** taxes **C.** preoccupation **D.** revenue
12. **A.** developer **B.** politician **C.** trickster **D.** antagonist
13. **A.** pinched **B.** cornered **C.** managed **D.** spread
14. **A.** eliminated **B.** wasted **C.** killed **D.** encouraged
15. **A.** attacked **B.** profited **C.** capitulated **D.** obliged
16. **A.** Attached **B.** Situated **C.** Fixed **D.** Separated
17. **A.** promised **B.** generated **C.** ensured **D.** demanded
18. **A.** border **B.** conservativeness **C.** confines **D.** boredom
19. **A.** grew **B.** flowered **C.** crumbled **D.** flourished
20. **A.** legacy **B.** memory **C.** personality **D.** generosity

B. Fill the gaps in the following sentences with the correct answer A, B C or D.

21 David is married to Mary, so he is her _____ .
   a eyesore **b** fiance **c** plasma **d** spouse
22 A spider spins a _____ .
   a lace **b** fare **c** yarn **d** web
23 Nobody lives here. It's a very _____ place.
   a desolate **b** perpetual **c** boisterous **d** responsive
24 Nobody likes teaching that _____ class.
   a responsible **b** quiet **c** boisterous **d** responsive
25 You must try to _____ your money more sensibly.
   a advocate **b** adapt **c** accommodate **d** budget
26 That little man goes unnoticed in the street, but he _____ immense power.
   a swings **b** handles **c** wields **d** practices
27 It isn't easy to make friends with him, he puts up a _____ between himself and other people.
   a barrier **b** barricade **c** border **d** boundary
28 We're at a loose end; we're going through a(n) _____ period in business right now.
   a slack **b** dearth **c** fast **d** indolent
29 The book was cheaper than I had _____ .
   a surveyed **b** anticipated **c** insisted **d** preserved
30 David looked _____ clumsy in his attempt to attract attention.
   a fancifully **b** oddly **c** absurdly **d** reasonably